NEW
CR[illegible]S
and healing stones

NEW CRYSTALS and healing stones

A complete guide to 150 recently available crystals and stones

JUDY HALL

A GODSFIELD BOOK
www.godsfield.co.uk

An Hachette Livre UK Company

First published in Great Britain in 2006 by
Godsfield Press, a division of Octopus Publishing Group Ltd
2–4 Heron Quays, London E14 4JP

ISBN-13: 978-1-84181-340-0
ISBN-10: 1-84181-340-0

A CIP catalogue record for this book is available from the British Library

Printed and bound in China

10 9 8 7 6 5 4 3 2 1

Disclaimer
The information given in this book is not intended to act as a substitute for medical treatment, nor can it be used for diagnosis. Crystals are powerful and are open to misunderstanding or abuse. If you are in any doubt about their use, a qualified practitioner should be consulted, especially in the crystal-healing field.

Contents

Index of Crystals

Introduction

Since my first books on crystals were written, many new stones have come on to the market and previously rare crystals are now available owing to new sources opening up. I have found further properties for one or two crystals. Mine-owners are looking carefully at stones before sending them to the crusher, and the lower levels of established mines are revealing unique combinations not previously seen. Amended or regrown crystals, some of which are extremely powerful, are increasing in popularity. New and rare stones can be found in crystal shops and on line, with mineral suppliers and mine galleries offering their best examples for sale at reasonable prices.

This book introduces the properties of these new stones, colours and forms. Many have an extremely high vibration and are seen by crystal workers as coming into prominence at this time to bring multidimensional healing, raising the vibration of the Earth and all who live upon it.

The word 'crystal' has been adopted by crystal healers to cover all stones and metals that have healing properties, not just gemstones. Healing is the term used to describe the beneficial effect of crystals, but it does not necessarily imply that stones will cure a condition.

Crystals deal with subtle dis-ease and emotional imbalances, bringing body, mind, emotions and spirit back into harmony and supporting the organs – in other words, providing holistic healing and bringing about increased vitality and well-being.

Pyrophyllite

Septarian egg

Using Your Crystals

Crystals work best when purified and attuned to your unique vibrations. Purify and attune a crystal as soon as you buy it, and cleanse each time it is handled. If you wear a crystal, cleanse it daily, especially if you are using it for healing.

Wash non-fragile crystals in running water to cleanse them.

Cleansing Crystals

To cleanse tumbled crystals, simply hold under running water for a few minutes and then place them in sun or bright light for a few hours to re-energize. To cleanse delicate, faceted or layered stones, cover with brown rice overnight and then place in the sun to re-energize, or place on a large Quartz cluster or Carnelian. Many white crystals enjoy the light of the full moon. Purpose-made crystal cleansers can be sprayed on to the crystal to cleanse and transmute the energies instantly.

Activating Crystals

Activating your crystal starts it working and attunes it to your unique energies, or to the person for whom it is intended. (While you can attune crystals for other people, it is always more beneficial for them to activate their own.)

To activate your crystal, hold your crystal and close your eyes. Concentrate on the crystal, seeing it surrounded by bright white light. Ask that the crystal be blessed by the

Hold your crystal in your hand to activate and focus it.

highest energies in the universe and be dedicated to your self-healing, and that of the environment around you, now or at any time in the future.

You can also use the activation to programme a crystal to carry out a specific task such as attracting abundance or love or sending healing.

Storing Crystals

Tumbled stones do not easily scratch so stones can be kept together in a cloth bag and a Carnelian added to cleanse and re-energize them. Other crystals should be kept wrapped separately, or displayed, but be aware that the colour of your crystals may fade in strong sunlight.

Silver spirals are excellent for wearing a crystal. Alternatively, it can be popped into a pocket, or kept on your desk or by your bed. Remember that crystals, whether worn or in the environment, will absorb negative energies and require regular cleansing.

Using your Crystals

Crystals can be used purely for decoration, although they will send subtle vibrations into the environment, regenerating the energies. They can be used to support an organ, change an ingrained attitude or emotional response, draw stagnant energy or trauma out of your body and improve well-being. The new stones work particularly well to reprogramme cellular memory from a previous life and clear the resulting dis-ease in the present. Healing is a subtle readjustment of

Wearing a crystal in a spiral is a useful way of accessing the benefits.

energies and attitudes to create greater harmony and vitality.

Healing crystals work differently on each individual body and some crystals will suit you and others not, especially high-vibration crystals or different colours of the same stone. You will tend to be attracted to crystals that are good for you and repelled by those that are not. However, because you may subconsciously resist a crystal that would work on unacknowledged issues, it may be better to dowse (see below) to ask if a crystal would be beneficial. Dowsing would also indicate the length of time it should be left in place.

Healing crystals can be placed over an organ, the site of pain or disease, or an appropriate chakra, and may be used on the body or in the aura (high-vibration stones often work best held a few centimetres away from the physical body). Placed over the thymus (higher heart chakra), a crystal will support or stimulate the immune system. If your crystal has a point or is wand-shaped, use it point outward from the body to draw off stagnant energy, pain or dis-ease; or point inward to re-energize and channel healing energy to the body. For chronic conditions, wear or tape a crystal in place for several hours and repeat at regular intervals. For other conditions, 10–20 minutes should be sufficient but if the crystal falls off or you begin to feel tired, you should stop using the crystal immediately.

Placing crystals while you are in a relaxed, meditative state is beneficial. Take a few slow deep breaths before you begin, letting go of any tension you feel and bringing your attention deep inside yourself.

How to Finger-dowse

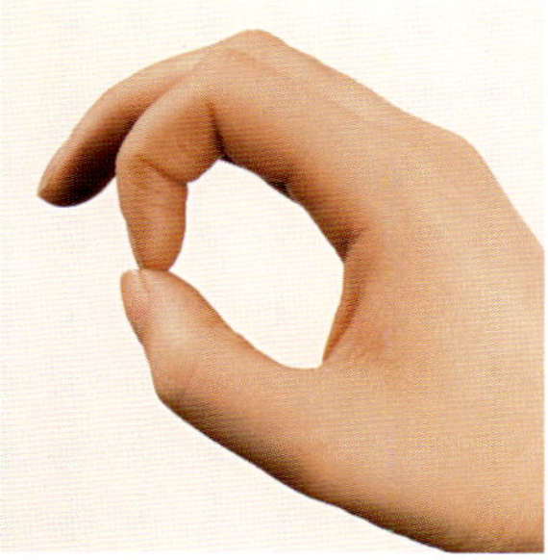

1 *Loop your thumb and finger together as shown.*

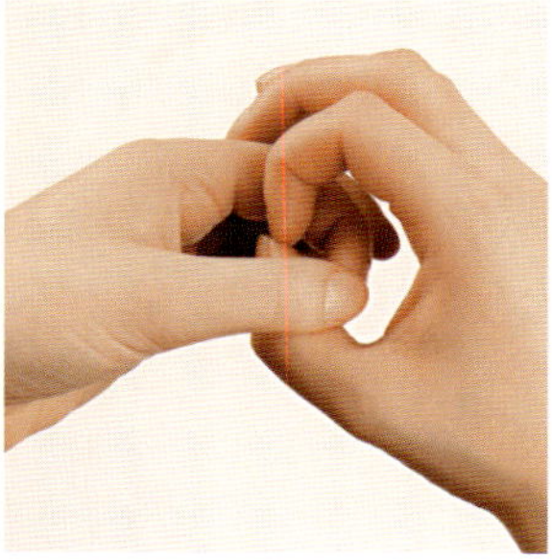

2 *Slip your other thumb and finger through the loop and close together. Hold over a crystal or photograph. Ask your question.*

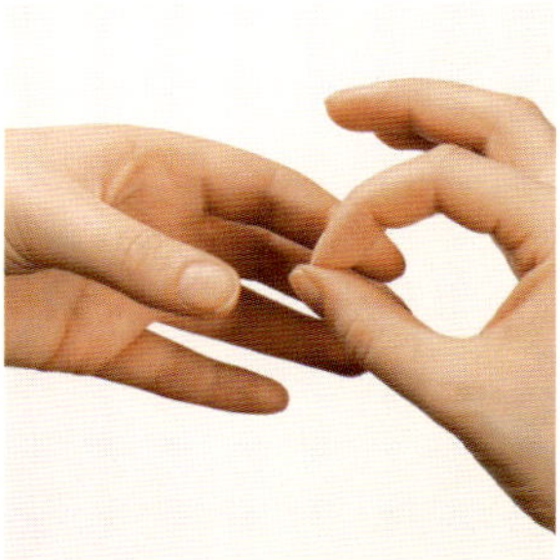

3 *Pull steadily. If the loop breaks, the answer to your question is no. If the loop holds, the answer to your question is yes.*

Crystal Healing

Where appropriate, each crystal entry includes the chakra or chakras associated with that stone. To use a crystal for healing through the chakra system, lie down and relax, and place it over the appropriate chakra, leaving in place for 20 minutes or so.

The Chakras

1 **Earth** Between the feet, linkage point to the earth

2 **Base** At the perineum, sexual and creative centre

3 **Sacral** Just below the navel

4 **Solar plexus** Emotional centre

5 **Spleen** Under left armpit, potential site of energy leakage

6 **Heart** Over the physical heart, love centre

7 **Higher heart** Over the thymus, centre of immunity

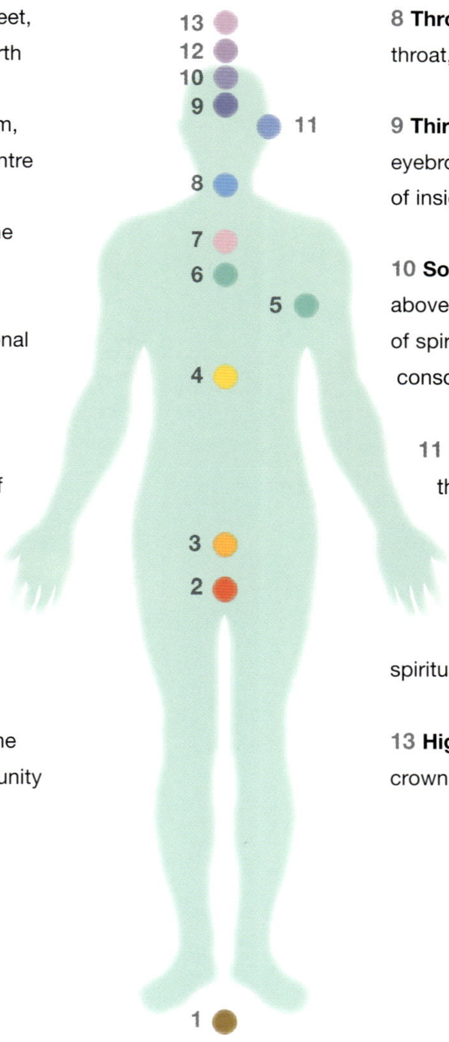

8 **Throat** Over the physical throat, centre of truth

9 **Third eye** Midway between eyebrows and hairline, centre of insight

10 **Soma** At the hairline above the third eye, centre of spiritual identity and consciousness activation

11 **Past life** Just behind the ears, stores past-life information

12 **Crown** At the top of the head, spiritual connection point

13 **Higher crown** Above the crown, linkage point for spirit

High-vibration Stones

Many new crystals have high vibrations that bring about multidimensional healing but these only work if your own vibrations are in harmony with the stone. If a crystal does not appear to work for you, hold it and gently concentrate on your palm. You may feel a tingle and your body will shift slightly as it attunes to the crystal. If so, persevere, sitting for ten minutes a day until the crystal begins to work. If not, choose another crystal. A high-vibration crystal may bring about a strong reaction or healing challenge. If this occurs, remove the crystal immediately and hold a Green Phantom or Smoky Quartz point down toward your feet to facilitate the release of energy out of your body. Wait a day or two before using the high-vibration crystal again.

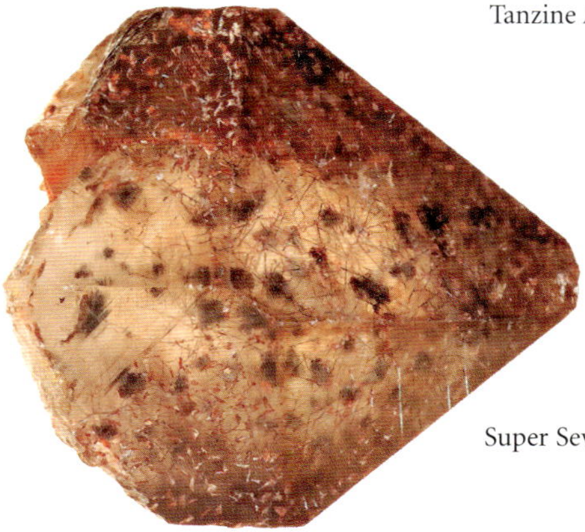

Super Seven

Tanzine Aura Quartz

Ajoite

Phantom Quartz (Desirite)

Gem Elixirs

As crystals work by vibration and resonance, energy can easily be transferred into spring water where it is stored until required.

A gem elixir is an excellent way to gently transfer the new crystal vibrations to the auric field, which is dispersed around the body about a hands breadth out.

How to Make a Gem Elixir

Cleanse your crystal and place in a clean glass bowl. Cover with pure spring water. (If the crystal is toxic or fragile, place in a clean glass bowl placed in a bowlful of spring water.) Leave in the sun for 6–12 hours. Remove the crystal. Bottle the water in a clean glass bottle and store in a refrigerator.

How to Use the Elixir

Sip the elixir at regular intervals, rub on the skin, or bathe affected part. If the elixir is to be kept more than a day, add one-third brandy or cider vinegar as a preservative. A few drops of gem elixir can also be used in your bath, or added to a spray bottle of water and spritzed around your home or workspace.

THE NEW CRYSTALS DIRECTORY

In the pages that follow, you will find descriptions and properties of the new stones and healing crystals. Where appropriate, their related chakra, number, zodiac sign and planet are also listed, but please note that in some cases these have yet to be determined or are not relevant.

Some of the stones are specific varieties or colours of a generic crystal such as Quartz or Jasper, which take myriad forms and generic information is included. Cross-references have been included where relevant to enable you to find the properties of the components of a combination stone.

Many entries have a section detailing organs and systems of the body for which the crystal is beneficial, conditions or negative feelings it heals, and positive attitudes it promotes. Some crystals work at a spiritual level, opening higher chakras, and do not necessarily have a physical healing application. Many work through the chakras and can be placed over a chakra to cleanse and align it and the organs or feelings with which it is associated.

The illustrations will assist you to identify your crystals and a comprehensive index will help you to locate the right crystal for your needs.

White Spirit Quartz

Properties White Spirit Quartz is an exceedingly spiritual stone that embodies all the energetic properties of Quartz, a master healer and powerful energy amplifier. Quartz multidimensionally regulates, purifies, absorbs, stores, releases and unblocks energy, making it a useful receptor for programmes and a dissolver of karmic patterns. Radiating high-vibration energy out in all directions, the core crystal tightly focuses healing and reprogrammes cellular memory. Enhancing metaphysical abilities, Spirit Quartz assists at death, guiding the soul through different dimensions of the afterlife to the highest possible vibration and into the hands of those who are waiting to welcome it home. It comforts those who are left behind and can be programmed for ancestral healing. Helpful in dream and metaphysical work, this crystal is beneficial in past-life healing as it rejigs the etheric blueprint for the present life. Pinpointing significant karmic connections and the gift or karmic justice in traumatic situations, it promotes self-forgiveness.

Beneficial for Group work, ascension, service, metaphysical abilities, multidimensional healing, cellular memory, rebirthing, enhancing brainwave synchronicity, blending yin/yang, purifying and stimulating the auric bodies, healing discord, patience, astral projection, detoxification, obsessive behaviour, fertility, skin eruptions.

Natural formation

Appearance	Chakra	Number	Zodiac sign
Drusy crystals covering a long point	Crown, cleanses all	6	All

Citrine Spirit Quartz

Properties One of the stones of abundance, joyful Citrine is a powerful cleanser and regenerator with a warming action. Never needing cleansing, it is excellent for environmental and auric protection. Imparting self-confidence and motivation, Citrine teaches how to go with the flow. Citrine Spirit Quartz, is a combination of Citrine and Quartz (see page 18). It brings about purification of intent and is particularly useful for accessing abundance while at the same time releasing any dependence on, or attachment to, material things. Promoting self-awareness, it purifies and cleanses the aura. Citrine Spirit Quartz assists you to stand centred in your power and to direct your life from that place. In business, it focuses your goals and plans. Used in grids, Citrine Spirit Quartz protects a house against electromagnetic smog or geopathic stress and heals disturbed earth energies. Citrine Spirit Quartz assists in conflict resolution and can be programmed to send forgiveness to those you feel have wronged you, or to ask for forgiveness.

Natural formation

Appearance	Chakra	Zodiac sign
Tiny, yellow-brown with clear or Amethyst crystals on a long point	Earth, solar plexus	Leo

Amethyst Spirit Quartz

Properties Compassionate Amethyst Spirit Quartz carries the vibration of Quartz (see page 18). Amethyst is a highly spiritual and extremely protective and calming stone that focuses the mind and is an excellent emotional balancer. Compassionate and selfless, Amethyst Spirit Quartz facilitates transition to other states of being and accessing higher consciousness. At the higher crown chakras it brings about transmutation of prior misuses of spiritual power, facilitating multidimensional healing including soul parts not in incarnation. It can be programmed to assist from afar a soul who is facing death – and offers immense support and comfort throughout a terminal illness.

Amethyst Spirit Quartz makes an excellent carrier for flower essences to gently dissolve karma, attitudes and emotions that would be detrimental if taken into the next world. An effective tool for spirit releasement, it encourages a trapped soul to move toward the light, attracting guides for the journey. Holding the stone enables a practitioner to journey safely wherever may be necessary to release the soul and to ascertain whether there is anything that the soul needs completing before it moves on.

Natural formation

Appearance	Chakra	Zodiac sign
Tiny Amethyst crystals covering a long point	Higher crown	Pisces

Smoky Spirit Quartz

Properties In addition to strongly protective, grounding and cleansing properties, Smoky Spirit Quartz carries the energy of Quartz (see page 18).

It promotes multidimensional cellular healing and integration. This stone is a most effective psychopomp, conveying the soul safely to the next world. As it does so, it cleanses the subtle bodies, removing layers of karmic and emotional debris to reprogramme cellular memory, ensuring a good rebirth. In a similar way, it is beneficial for any work that entails visiting the underworld or exploring the subconscious mind as it cleanses and releases deeply held emotions and states of dis-ease or traumatic memories, including those that have passed down the ancestral line. Such work may need to be under the guidance of a practitioner as it may create catharsis.

Smoky Spirit Quartz can be used to stabilize and purify areas of environmental imbalance or pollution, no matter what the cause.

Natural formation

Appearance	Chakra	Zodiac sign
Tiny greyish-brown crystals covering a long point	Base, third eye	Scorpio

Flame Aura Spirit Quartz

Properties Created from Titanium and Niobium, Flame Aura Spirit Quartz brings about a profound multidimensional energy shift, drawing kundalini energy up the spine and through all the subtle bodies. This crystal mediates its effect to provide what each individual soul needs for its evolution. With its powerful violet emanation, it harmonizes all the rays and the astrological chart. This stone assists you to 'read' people. Flame Aura Spirit Quartz is a powerful initiation tool. Flame Aura is also available in non-spirit Quartz which, as a wand, has the same properties.

Flame Aura Spirit Quartz

Flame Aura Quartz wand

Appearance
Multi-coloured coating on Spirit Quartz

Fairy Quartz

Properties Fairy Quartz is a less ethereal stone than Spirit Quartz (see page 18), the crystals along the laser point being tiny and less prominent and its vibrations more earthly, but it nevertheless carries the vibration of Spirit Quartz. Rather than high spiritual dimensions, it links into the Faery kingdom and contacts planetary and Earth devas, assisting you to unravel your family myths, and the ancestral or cultural stories in which you are locked, and reframe these where appropriate.

This is a useful stone for families as it soothes the home environment, removes emotional pain and quietens children after nightmares. Fairy Quartz can be used as a wand to draw out emotional or physical dis-ease or to introduce healing energy into the body, especially that of a child. This stone is perfect for programming to manifest the desires of your creative inner child.

Beneficial for Detoxifying tissues, drawing off pain.

Natural formation

Appearance	Number	Zodiac sign
Long opaque point with tiny crystals forming chains	9	Gemini

Orange Drusy Quartz

Properties Drusy Quartz carries the powerful vibration of Quartz and Spirit Quartz (see page 18) and is found in several colours. Ideal for the bedridden and for carers, Orange Drusy Quartz fosters harmony, making it easier to offer and receive help, and to show thankfulness and appreciation. This stone increases compassion and instils the ability to laugh at life in the most difficult circumstances. Kept in your pocket, or placed by the bedside, it energizes and invigorates your whole body.

Beneficial for Self-imposed limitations, revitalization, periodontal disease, lethargy.

Drusy Quartz on a matrix

Appearance	Chakra	Zodiac sign
Tiny orange-red crystals on a matrix	Base and sacral	Aries

Bushman Red Cascade Quartz

Properties The colour in Bushman Quartz comes from Limonite (see page 96), creating a powerful energetic charge that allows you to draw on deep reserves of energy, physical and emotional. A few minutes with this highly energetic stone quickly invigorates you, taking you to a high energetic level, but it needs to be used with caution as the energies may be too much to handle unless you are skilled in working with crystals; for this reason, this stone is best used under the direction of a qualified crystal therapist. Enhancing skill and efficiency, Bushman Quartz can be programmed to bring about a favourable legal outcome.

Beneficial for Positive action, persistence, vitality, vigour, blood flow, blood vessels, muscles.

Natural form

Appearance	Chakra	Zodiac sign
Drusy Quartz cascading down a large point	Base and sacral	Aries

Fenster Quartz

Properties Fenster Quartz is an excellent tool for sending healing light and for energy work that requires a high vibration. The natural etched triangle formations within the planes of Fenster Quartz can be traversed as an inner landscape for insight or meditation. This stone stimulates clairvoyance (clear-seeing) and assists in healing dysfunctional patterns and outgrown emotions. It throws light on the past-life or childhood causes of addiction and assists in removing them, letting go the need for 'more' that so often leads to obsessions and compulsions of all kinds, and reprogramming cellular memory. It is also beneficial for conditions such as obsessive compulsive disorder or Tourette's Syndrome.

Beneficial for Eyes, addictions, eating disorders, obsessive compulsive disorder, tics and spasms.

Natural form

Appearance	Chakra	Zodiac sign
Inner windows in Clear Quartz	All	Aquarius

Sugar Blade Quartz

Properties Sugar Blade Quartz is the stone for extra-terrestrial and star contact, said to encourage spaceship landings if gridded around a site. If you wish to share the teachings of our neighbours in the universe, or to know which star you hail from, Sugar Blade Quartz takes you to a place of communication and connection. If you wish to know about your own true Self, place Sugar Blade Quartz on the soma chakra. It will help you attune to the breadth of your core spiritual identity and reflect this out to the world. Sugar Blade Quartz carries the life force energy and a hologram of your multidimensional bodies. It aligns to and engages with the 'I am' principle and can assist in choosing a life direction, showing which door to open.

Appearance	Chakra	Zodiac sign
Long blades on the side of Drusy Quartz	Soma	Aquarius

Star Hollandite Inclusion Quartz

Properties Bringing together the energies of Quartz (see page 18) and Goethite (see page 123), Star Hollandite brings a depth and stillness to meditation that takes you into the oneness of all things. It is an excellent stone if you want to stimulate contact with the stars, star beings, star lore or universal wisdom. This stone can take you back to view the origins of ancient Egypt and the intervention of the star people in its development. This stone also assists rational thought and helps to disperse tension and anxiety. Drawing off negative energy at the physical and mental levels, it brings about a state of calm acceptance and inner watchfulness.

Natural form

Appearance	Chakra
Tiny six-pointed stars included within a Quartz point	Balances all

Starseed Quartz

Properties Starseed is reputed to be the perfect crystal for galactic and interdimensional communication. It is also said to put you in close touch with the ancient civilization of Lemuria. Peppered with indentations that look like a star map, Starseed assists in discovering which star your spirit is associated with. Like an etched crystal, Starseed can be read to rediscover ancient knowledge and your purpose in incarnating. Starseed carries Green Tara energy and can take you to a Shamballah-like state of awareness that carries exceptional clarity and goes to pure form. It connects and realigns to the blueprint that informs the etheric blueprint. Used in conjunction with Sugar Blade Quartz it activates the unmanifest, bringing heart and soul into perfect unity.

Natural form

Appearance	Chakra
Deeply etched on alternate faces, or may have Drusy Quartz on one face and etching on another	Higher crown

Shift Crystal

Properties A form of Quartz (see page 18) laid down on Calcite, which later dissolved leaving blades and spaces to be traversed, and said by some to be formed where the tectonic plates of the Earth collide, a Shift Crystal does exactly what the name suggests: it shifts you into a new space and accelerates your spiritual growth. It is the perfect stone to take into meditation or to place under your pillow at night but you need to be ready to take whatever a Shift Crystal offers. There is no going back with this crystal and its effects can be dramatic, traumatic and overwhelming as it shifts you onto your soul path, opens healing potential, and clears the evolutionary way forward. Other stones may be needed to help assimilate the changes it creates in your life.

A Shift Crystal can greatly amplify Reiki healing, strengthening healer and patient, and can be programmed to carry the symbols during and after a session or to reprogramme cellular memory.

Natural form

Appearance	Chakra	Zodiac sign	Planet
Multi-faceted, bladed and indented with inner spaces	Heart, higher heart, third eye, crown and higher crown	Aquarius	Uranus

Faden Quartz

Properties Faden Quartz enhances self-healing and personal growth, purifies the aura and harmonizes chakra energy flow. Excellent for communication during the healing process, Faden Quartz unifies the Self, encouraging fragmented soul parts to reintegrate. When working at a distance, Faden Quartz connects healer and patient. The thread simulates the 'silver cord' attaching the etheric body to the physical during out-of-body experiences, and protects during journeying. Faden Quartz provides a link to the higher self when seeking answers. Helpful during past-life regression, especially between lives, it overviews soul lessons and root causes of dis-ease.

A gap-bridger, this crystal attunes the energies of a group, particularly if the intention is to heal something 'broken' or overcome conflict. If you are suffering from intense internal trauma, Faden Quartz gives you strength to overcome. It can be used to grid areas of unstable earth or physical energy.

Beneficial for Emotional instability, breaks and fractures, stability at all levels, cellular memory, removing cysts and encrustations, back pain, inner alignment.

Natural form

Appearance	Chakra	Zodiac sign
Clear flat crystal, distinctive thread-like line running through it	Opens all, especially crown and past life	Libra, Scorpio

Apple Aura Quartz

Properties Apple Aura Quartz is created when nickel is bonded onto Quartz (see page 18). Apple Aura Quartz is an excellent protector for the spleen when worn over the base of the sternum, or taped over the spleen chakra, as it cuts multidimensional energy drains and overcomes the psychic vampirism created when someone draws on your energies without permission. It can also assist in cutting ties with previous partners or mentors who retain a powerful mental or emotional hold.

Long point

Appearance	Chakra
Apple-green iridescent clear crystal	Spleen

Tanzine Aura Quartz

Properties A mystical new Aura Quartz alchemicalized from Indium, a rare metal that falls at the centre of the periodic table, Tanzanite brings about multidimensional balance. Opening and aligning the highest crown chakras way above the subtle bodies, this delicate crystal draws cosmic energy into the physical body and to Earth. It has a powerful regulatory effect on the pituitary, hypothalamus and pineal glands, bringing about profound spiritual interconnection and physical equilibrium.

The properties of Tanzine are still being fully explored but it is known that Indium, used as a homoeopathic remedy for many years, assists the assimilation of minerals, bringing about optimal metabolic and hormonal balance, resulting in physical and mental well-being, and is believed to be anti-carcinogenic. This stone would appear to be excellent for overcoming the effects of thyroid, spleen and mineral deficiency.

Beneficial for Metabolism, migraine, mineral assimilation, insomnia, attention deficit disorder, immune system, convalescence, depression, inflammation, fibromyalgia, lupus, diabetes, vision, glaucoma, urinary tract, blood pressure, circulation, pneumonia, pancreas, spleen, liver.

Short point

Appearance	Chakra	Number	Zodiac sign
Iridescent bluish-lavender Clear Quartz point or cluster	Higher crown, opens and aligns all	8	Virgo–Pisces

Green Siberian Quartz

Properties Regrown in Russia from natural Quartz (see page 18) combined with chemicals, Green Siberian Quartz is an extremely powerful stone that brings in a strong love vibration to heal the heart and emotions. This stone is particularly useful when worn to harmonize disputes, such as arguments with neighbours, or at meetings between people who have opposing points of views. Said to create prosperity and abundance, it is considered to be a lucky stone for matters of health, love and money.

Beneficial for Heart, emotions, lung conditions, altitude sickness.

Appearance	Chakra
Clear green Quartz	Heart

Shaped piece

Gold Siberian Quartz

Properties Gold Siberian Quartz stimulates the solar plexus and increases willpower and the ability to bring your creative vision into positive manifestation. Programme it to bring you all that your heart desires and to dissolve former misuse of will or aggression that has had karmic effects.

Shaped piece

Appearance	Chakra
Clear gold Quartz	Solar plexus

Purple Siberian Quartz

Properties A stone for the spiritual magician, Purple Siberian Quartz helps you to co-create your own reality and to keep yourself centred and grounded during ritual or spiritual working. It is a powerful stimulant for the third eye and higher crown chakras, leading to mystical states of consciousness at the very highest levels.

Shaped piece

Appearance	Chakra
Clear purple Quartz	Crown and higher crown

Blue Siberian Quartz

Properties Mystical Blue Siberian Quartz, alchemicalized from cobalt, brings about intense visionary experiences and opens you to an influx of cosmic consciousness. The crystal stimulates psychic vision and telepathy, and enhances communication, lifting the spirit and instilling deep peace. It assists you in speaking your truth and facilitates being heard.

Beneficial for Throat infections (as an elixir gargle), stomach ulcers, stress, depression, inflammation, sunburn, stiff neck or muscles.

Appearance	Chakra
Clear bright-blue Quartz	Throat, third eye, crown

Shaped piece

Actinolite Quartz

Properties Actinolite Quartz is particularly useful if you feel you have lost your way and are looking for a new direction. Instilling a sense of right timing, it shows you the new path you should take for constructive evolution, and helps you to see the value in your mistakes. See Actinolite, page 116.

Beneficial for Detoxification, metabolism.

Natural

Appearance
Blackish or green threads or phantom in clear Quartz

Chinese Chromium Quartz

Properties A manufactured Quartz, created by superheating Quartz with the mineral Chromium so that it fuses on the surface. So far, few specific properties have been identified except those below.

Beneficial for Mobilization of heavy metal out of the body, blood sugar imbalances, chronic fatigue, weight regulation, hormone deficiencies.

Amended cluster

Appearance
Bubbly coating on points and 'tubes'

Ouro Verde Quartz

Properties Created by bombarding Quartz with gamma rays, Ouro Verde means 'green gold' and is reputed to put you in touch with the deeper meaning of life and allow you to view future events in the light of wisdom from the past, leading to more productive choices. Said to have a high energy that never requires cleansing or recharging and giving powerful protection to the user, some people feel nauseous when touching it and sensitive people may have a strong adverse reaction, describing it as 'a sledge hammer to crack a nut'.

More positively, it is seen as holding the symbolism of an Olympic torch, taking the world forward into brotherhood and cooperation. For people who are not averse, it actualizes abundance and 'seasons the character' to enable them to shine. Ouro Verde is reported to detect triggers for illness and radon gas, and to protect against radioactivity.

Beneficial for Tumours, herpes, allergies, anaphylactic shock, peripheral circulation, Reynaud's disease.

Raw

Appearance	Chakra	Number	Zodiac sign
Slightly oily or cracked olive green Quartz	Third eye, crown	1	Leo

Pink Crackle Quartz

Properties Crackle Quartz has been superheated and cyed and this flirty crystal promotes fun and joy in life. An excellent companion for life-enhancing pursuits that help you to recharge, it is a useful adjunct to Reiki healing, facilitating contact with your higher self. This stone can also be used to heal an abused or emotionally damaged child. It is very good at helping you to love your body, no matter what size, shape and age it is, and is excellent for accepting who you are in your entirety. Programme it to attract love.

Beneficial for Pancreas, diabetes, cellular memory, brittle bones, compound fractures, anxiety, earwax, pain experienced during flying owing to pressure in the ears.

Pillar

Appearance	Chakra	Zodiac sign
Clear Quartz crystal cracked and crazed inside	Solar plexus and heart	Libra

Sichuan Quartz

Properties Energetically combining the powerful vibrations of Herkimer and Tibetan Quartz, and carrying an extremely high, sparky vibration, this natural Chinese Quartz rapidly opens psychic and inner vision. Harmonizing the subtle bodies with the physical, it bridges energy gaps along the chakra line. As with Tibetan Quartz, this rarified stone has a grounded and centred energy that passes into the body and the personal self, bringing about deep healing of the aura and etheric blueprint from which the present physical body devolved. It energizes and harmonizes the meridians.

Beneficial and insightful if held by a healer or past-life therapist while working with a client, it accesses the Akashic Record, putting you in touch with ancient Chinese wisdom or highlighting the past-life reasons for dis-ease or karmic lessons being dealt with in the present life. Double-terminated Black Phantom Quartz (see page 62) from Virginia carries very similar energy to Sichuan Quartz.

Beneficial for Energy meridians, cellular memory, eating disorders, breaking dependent or co-dependent relationships, centring in one's Self.

Natural double termination

Appearance	Chakra	Zodiac sign
Double-terminated, very Clear Quartz, may have black spot inclusions	All, connects third eye and crown	Virgo

Amethyst Herkimer

Properties Herkimers are strongly energetic stones that facilitate creativity and conscious attunement to the highest spiritual dimensions, stimulating the opening of spiritual gifts. Blocking geopathic or electromagnetic stress, they are excellent gridding stones. Fine-tuning the third eye and carrying the protective and spiritually opening vibration of Amethyst, Amethyst Herkimer is a powerful metaphysical tool that facilitates soul retrieval from any lifetime, inducing deep core soul healing, and integrating all the disparate parts of the Self. Freeing the incarnated soul of its karmic burdens and aligning with other soul dimensions to cohere the soul as a vehicle for spirit, Amethyst Herkimers can bring about profound spiritual evolution and altered states of consciousness.

As with all Herkimers, this stone links two people together when parted and enhances telepathy. It creates a powerful soul shield when journeying or meditating, and restores and purifies energy after undertaking spiritual or healing work. It is perfect for programming to attract your twinflame and soul companions.

Amethyst Herkimer on matrix

Appearance	Chakra	Zodiac sign
Ghostly Amethyst phantoms or inclusion in a bright double-terminated clear crystal	Higher heart and higher crown, third eye	Pisces

'Citrine' Herkimer

Properties Stained by yellow oil giving the appearance of Citrine, 'Citrine' Herkimer clears away poverty-consciousness and the ingrained programmes and beliefs that keep you mired in poverty, opening the way to abundance and enhancing motivation. A powerful cleanser and regenerator, this is an excellent stone for enhancing earth energies, making them sparkle, and for encouraging the ethical harvesting of the riches and resources of the environment. Placed in the ground, 'Citrine' Herkimer purifies the creative force and encourages abundant fertility in all that grows. Worn around the neck, 'Citrine' Herkimer is a powerful protector for the aura, subtle bodies and chakras. It can be helpful in cleansing and realigning cellular memory.

Natural large form

Appearance	Chakra	Zodiac sign
Yellow double-terminated clear crystal or cluster	Solar plexus, heart	Leo

Smoky Herkimer

Properties Smoky Herkimer is an excellent psychic clearing tool with powerful cleansing and detoxifying energies that clear the subtle and physical bodies. Smoky Herkimer is an earth healer.

Gridded around a building it protects against electromagnetic or geopathic pollution and draws its effects out of the subtle bodies.

A comfort for those who are approaching death, it gently absorbs negative energies and emotions that would be detrimental to the soul if carried into the next world, bringing in the karma of grace.

Natural form

Appearance	Chakra	Zodiac sign
Brownish-grey tinge to clear Herkimer	Earth and base	Scorpio

Golden Enhydro Herkimer

Properties Containing bubbles of liquid millions of years old, Enhydros symbolize the collective unconscious underlying and uniting everything. This stone brings about deep emotional healing and transmutation on all levels.

True Golden Enhydro Herkimer is a rare stone from the Himalayas that is incredibly energetic. An excellent developer of spiritual gifts that stimulates the third eye, clearing implants and removing restrictions placed on spiritual sight in this or any other life, it takes you straight to the ages-old wisdom of the sacred mountains. A powerful healer for the solar plexus and for emotional disturbances that have been carried over many lifetimes, Golden Enhydro cleanses the emotional body and blueprint, creating emotional well-being. This stone eliminates gender confusion or ambivalence in those who have changed sex from one incarnation to another.

Small double termination

Appearance	Chakra	Zodiac sign
Double-terminated crystals with small, clearly visible bubbles of yellow oil floating within	Solar plexus, third eye, crown and higher crown	Cancer–Leo

Blue Quartz (natural)

Properties Tranquil Blue Quartz assists in reaching out to others and inspires hope. Calming the mind, it assuages fear, assists in understanding your own spiritual nature and facilitates passing through a metamorphosis. This stone fires your creativity. Excellent if you suffer from disorganization, Blue Quartz instils mental clarity and self-discipline.

Natural Blue Quartz may have Aerinite, Dumortierite (see page 138), Rutile (see page 97) or Indicolite (see page 66) included within it and will encompass and amplify the qualities of these stones. See also Blue Phantom Quartz, page 61.

Beneficial for Organs in upper body, detoxification, depression, bloodstream, throat, immune system, overstimulation, spleen, endocrine system. If Blue Quartz is rutilated, it is believed to restrain premature ejaculation.

Raw crystals on a matrix

Appearance	Chakra	Number	Zodiac sign
Clear blue Quartz or patches included in Quartz	Throat	44	Taurus

Lavender Quartz

Properties Lavender Quartz raises the vibration of the gently loving emotional healer Rose Quartz to an even higher spiritual love connection. An excellent stimulator for metaphysical gifts and for interdimensional communication, it takes meditation to a new high.

A stone of self-remembering and heightened self-awareness, it enables recall of what you do in all dimensions of consciousness and reintegrates the vast spectrum of your spiritual Self.

Lavender Quartz brings about profound emotional and multidimensional healing for body and soul.

Beneficial for Brainwave and brain-frequency disharmonies, cellular regeneration.

Raw

Appearance	Chakra	Zodiac sign
Opaque to clear lilac Quartz	Heart, throat, brow and higher crown	Pisces

Smoky Rose Quartz

Properties This unusual combination brings together the unconditionally loving generic energy of Rose Quartz, with its ability to promote deep emotional healing and instil trust, with the cleansing and protective energies of Smoky Quartz. Smoky Rose Quartz dissolves resentment and draws out detrimental effects of abuse, filling the heart with unconditional love and providing a protective shield to allow healing to continue.

This beautiful stone keeps your environment pure, quickly transmuting negative energy and replacing it with love. The perfect stone to accompany anyone who is frightened of death or dying, it should be placed by the bed or under the pillow.

Raw

Appearance	Chakra	Zodiac sign
Opaque or clear pink Quartz with smoky points or inclusions	Heart and higher heart	Libra–Scorpio

Smoky Citrine

Properties One of the few stones that never requires cleaning, Smoky Citrine does not hold negative energy, instantly transmuting it. This stone is excellent for enhancing psychic abilities and grounding them in everyday reality and for removing blockages from your spiritual path. It is a useful stone for removing vows taken in other lives, especially those of poverty and chastity. Smoky Citrine clears away any beliefs and thought forms that keep you mired in poverty, opening the way to abundance.

This stone purifies the etheric blueprint and removes the effects of detrimental attitudes from the past. This stone also assists you to move out of circumstances or an environment that does not allow you to expand.

Raw

Appearance	Chakra	Zodiac sign
Dark brownish-yellow patches within a citrine crystal	Earth and solar plexus	Leo, Scorpio

Smoky Amethyst

Properties Smoky Amethyst has a two-way charge that earths spiritual energy and allows access to the highest levels of awareness, focusing powerful energy into the body.

An extremely efficient stone for entity clearing, especially at the third eye, this gatekeeper protects against psychic attack and alien invasion, repelling negative energy while calling in positive and, placed on the soma chakra, attunes you to your pure spiritual Self. Clearing the higher heart chakra and opening the throat chakra, it facilitates expression of your own truth.

Raising your vibrations, shielding and screening you from background psychic interference, Smoky Amethyst holds a light while you are working in the shadows or underworld. It empowers you to shift ingrained past-life trauma or heal soul splits and reprogrammes cellular memory.

This stone contacts angelic helpers, assisting with disconnection between those who have previously made a mystic marriage and remain intertwined at the higher chakras. Smoky Amethyst gently disentangles energetic connections, sealing against reconnection.

Natural

Natural

Appearance	Chakra	Zodiac sign
Smoky Quartz and Amethyst combined in one crystal	Third eye, soma, past life, higher heart and throat	Scorpio

Strawberry Quartz

Properties Natural Strawberry Quartz is a rare crystal that makes a potent elixir for bringing love into the heart, creating a harmonious environment. Assisting in living consciously and joyfully in the moment, it sees the humour in all situations. Strawberry Quartz has an intense energy that assists dream recall. Stabilizing connections between the physical body and the aura, it keeps you connected, and brings to light hidden causes of current situations, especially when these are self-created. Lessening the restrictions you place upon yourself, it reprogrammes false beliefs and assists in positive affirmations.

Strawberry Quartz may be artificially manufactured, which lessens but does not negate the intensity of its action.

Beneficial for Anxiety, heart.

Raw

Tumbled

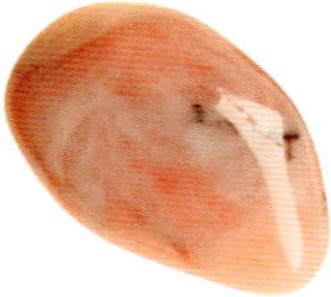

Appearance	Chakra	Zodiac sign
Clear to opaque Quartz or inclusions within Quartz	Heart	Libra

Vera Cruz Amethyst

Properties Vera Cruz Amethyst is said to instantly take you into a beta brainwave state, facilitating meditation, trance and spiritual journeying and enhancing divination skills. It is a powerful tool for shamanic working at high levels, facilitating access to the vibratory planes where souls meet and merge in oneness. A type of Amethyst, it can bring about profound interdimensional cellular healing.

Natural

Appearance	Chakra	Zodiac sign
Very light delicate Amethyst	All, especially third eye and crown or higher crown	Pisces

Brandenberg Amethyst

Properties Brandenberg Amethyst has a very old soul and an extremely high vibration. Emanating infinite compassion to all of creation, it is perfect for deep soul healing and forgiveness. An excellent aid to spiritual work at all levels, rapidly linking to multi-dimensions, this stone has a structure that is characterized by 'inner windows' or phantoms that assist in looking within. Placed on the soma chakra it attunes to your archetypal spiritual identity, facilitating true self-reflection and consciousness activation.

A Smoky Brandenberg, combining protective Amethyst and cleansing Smoky Quartz, is the finest tool available for removing implants, attachments, spirit possession or mental influence. This is the stone *par excellence* for conscious transformation or transition, especially through the death process as Smoky Quartz is one of the most efficient grounding and protective crystals that neutralizes negative energy of all kinds and teaches how to leave behind what no longer serves you.

Beneficial for Vitality, healing crisis, recovery from illness, radiation-related illness, chemotherapy, cellular memory, depletion, concussion, immune deficiencies, ME.

Natural points

Appearance	Chakra	Zodiac sign
Bright clear Quartz, Smoky Quartz or Amethyst, often with Amethyst and Smoky Quartz phantoms included within	Higher crown, soma, past life	Pisces

Elestial Quartz

Properties A stone of change and transformation, Elestial Quartz turns confusion into illumination and sets you on your life path. Connecting to the eternal Self, it links to the divine and higher planes of guidance, and opens spiritual gifts. Excellent for attuning to the eternal knowledge at the heart of the universe and within one's own soul, this crystal takes you into other lives to understand your karma or deep into your Self to give insight into evolutionary soul processes at work. It facilitates deep karmic release and brings about core soul healing and regenerates cellular memory.

Elestial Quartz's gently glowing energy removes blockages and fear, balancing polarities and opening the way to necessary change – which may come about abruptly. Sustaining and comforting, it overcomes emotional burdens.

Beneficial for Multidimensional cellular healing, regeneration, restructuring, spiritual evolution, self-healing, restoring brain cells after drug or alcohol abuse.

Natural

Appearance	Chakra	Zodiac sign
Clear or coloured Quartz with folds and terminations (often encompassed within an artificially shaped larger point)	Crown, bridges the flow of energy between all	Pisces

Amethyst Elestial

Properties Said to be a 'crystal of the angels', an Amethyst Elestial is a very powerful healing stone. It works on the higher chakras, stimulates the pineal gland, and opens a connection to interplanetary beings, guides and helpers. Amethyst Elestial shows you the relevance and effects of your past-life experiences on your present situation and removes resultant blockages. Dispersing negative energy from an alien or other source, it provides reassurance and calm. It is the perfect Elestial to support brain healing and ameliorate the effects of drugs or alcohol, and to bring about multi-dimensional and cellular memory healing.

Large Amethyst Elestials can be gridded around a healing room to enhance the energies and provide a safe space in which to work, but should be cleaned regularly.

Shaped point

Appearance	Chakra	Zodiac sign
Deep purple stone with folds and terminations (may be included within one large point often artificially shaped)	Higher crown and upwards	Pisces

Smoky Elestial

Properties Smoky Elestial contacts beneficial helpers in the spirit world to guard and guide you while you travel the multidimensional planes of existence. Protective, grounding and energetically cleansing, this intense stone takes you into past lives to reclaim your power, purify negativity and release from anyone who has enslaved you. It releases karmic curses or enmeshment and the effects of magical rituals that no longer serve. Particularly useful during reframing and past-life healing, it works equally well in present-life adjustments, creating profound mult-idimensional cellular healing, especially when combined with Amethyst.

A Smoky Elestial is an extremely efficient tool for mopping up negative energy and healing its effects, pulling past-life trauma out of the current physical body, and healing the etheric blueprint and aura. This stone cleanses and heals the ancestral line of trauma and emotional pain.

Shaped point

Appearance	Chakra	Zodiac sign
Smoky grey or brown with many folds and terminations, may be included within one large point	Base, cleanses all	Scorpio

Candle Quartz

Properties Said to be a light-bringer for the planet and those who have incarnated to assist Earth, and those upon it. To shift vibration, Candle Quartz highlights soul purpose and focuses your life path, assisting in putting ancient knowledge into practice and bringing your guardian angel closer. Candle Quartz can be programmed to attract spiritual abundance or to bring light into your home. If you find physical incarnation uncomfortable, Candle Quartz makes you feel good about your body.

This nurturing stone dissipates feelings of oppression and despair, promoting tranquillity and confidence and healing the heart. Candle Quartz is helpful in understanding how the physical body can be damaged by emotional or mental distress and reprogrammes cellular memory. Instilling clarity, it assists in looking within to find your truth and can be used as a scrying stone for personal illumination.

Beneficial for Self-image, converting carbohydrates and nutrients into energy, regulating insulin, headaches.

Natural soulmate points

Appearance	Chakra	Zodiac sign
Opaque point covered by melted wax	All	Taurus

Phantom Quartz

Properties Symbolizing universal awareness and the numerous lifetimes of the soul, Phantom facilitates transitions. A multi-layered Phantom takes you travelling through many dimensions or into your innermost self, stripping away the layers to reveal your core. Stimulating healing for the planet and rejigging detrimental landscape patterns, it activates healing ability. Accessing the Akashic Record, reading past lives and recovering repressed memories to put the past into context, Phantom takes you into the between-lives state to discover current soul plan and assess the next step, or to access healing the physical body through the etheric blueprint. A Phantom reconciles you to your shadow and integrates it.

Multi-layered White Phantom Quartz considerably expands transmission of light and information between higher realms and the Earth, opening the recipient to receive healing across immense distances. White Phantoms have been used for psychic surgery and to remove impacted layers of karma, opening the way for the karma of grace to operate and for cellular memory healing to occur.

Beneficial for Contacting guides, enhancing meditation, releasing ingrained patterns, hearing disorders, clairaudience.

'Shaman' Phantom Quartz

White Phantom

Appearance	Chakra
Ghostly crystal, triangles or patches of colour	Varies according to colour

Desirite

Properties A rare stone, Desirite has been designated the 'as above so below' stone, personifying the ancient astrological and alchemical doctrine of correspondence. This strongly grounding phantom nevertheless takes you to a very high vibration. Rubbing your thumb up the crystal takes you into profound meditative states; each level can be accessed successively, the Phantoms acting like lift stops. Desirite is excellent for angel and Ascended Master work and for accessing lives far back in the history of the planet. Resonating to the master number 44, it leads into metamorphosis and multi-dimensional transmutation, and a recognition of the interweaving of the divine with the spiritual.

Desirite does not work well as part of a healing layout – it is best used alone or to align and rebalance after a healing session or to facilitate cellular memory reframing.

Sliced point

Appearance	Chakra	Number
Clear Quartz with orange, brown, white and blue phantoms	All	44

Red Phantom Quartz

Properties Red Phantom Quartz is an inclusion of Limonite (see page 96), Hematite, Hematite-included (see page 68) and/or Kaolinite. A useful stone for removing energy implants and for healing 'gaps' in the aura, this phantom revitalizes the lower chakras and synthesizes these with the solar plexus to support creativity. Releasing emotional pain or past-life trauma, it heals emotional dysfunction. Red Phantom imparts tranquillity to your mind and energizes the physical body. It heals your inner child by allowing you to feel what had to be blocked out and repressed in childhood in order to survive, and to reconnect to your joy – additional stones may be required to heal the child fully.

Chinese Red Phantom, formed from Hematite, is an excellent stone for overcoming existential despair and restoring life force and vitality to the body. Helpful in business and enhancing financial security, this phantom induces perseverance and overcomes frustration. Used by knowledgeable Earth healers, it stabilizes the planet.

Natural formation

Appearance	Chakra	Zodiac sign
Solid red point or inclusion	Base, sacral, solar plexus	Aries

Orange Phantom Quartz

Properties Orange Phantom combines Quartz and Carnelian, an efficient cleanser and abundance attractor that overcomes abuse and protects and grounds you in present reality. Strongly energizing and rejuvenating, it overcomes an addictive personality, ending search for 'more' and focusing on recovery. It helps you to access who you really are. Once reconnected to this sense of Self, your insights can be put to work in everyday life.

Point

Appearance	Chakra	Zodiac sign
Solid or pyramidal inner crystal or patch of colour	Base and sacral, solar plexus, third eye, heart	Leo

Reversed Orange Phantom Quartz

Properties Formed when Carnelian fuses around Quartz that may be barely visible, Reversed Orange Phantom offers clarity into one's own inner workings and into the true meaning of the universe. Helpful in diagnosis as it takes you into the physical body to the site and subtle cause of dis-ease and addiction, it is useful when you need to take control of your life or require long-term sustenance and vitality.

Shaped point

Appearance	Chakra	Zodiac sign
Orange crystal around an inner clear core	Base and sacral	Leo

Yellow Phantom Quartz

Properties Yellow Phantom assists the mind to recall and reorganize memories and thought patterns. The inclusion is Limonite (see page 96), a stimulator for intellectual activities of all kinds. This Phantom efficiently removes mental attachments created in this life or any other.

Natural point

Appearance	Chakra	Zodiac sign
Ghostly yellow inner crystal or patch of colour	Third eye, crown, past life and solar plexus	Gemini

Smoky Phantom Quartz

Properties Smoky Phantom Quartz takes you to before you left your soul group. Attracting members of your soul group to fulfil your karmic or spiritual task, if negative energies have intervened in group purpose, it goes to original intention. Taking you to before a personal problem or pattern originated, reconnecting to wholeness, it also accesses shaman or wise-woman lives, activating your karmic wisdom.

Natural point

Appearance	Chakra	Zodiac sign
Phantom-like smoky point or inclusion within clear Quartz	Past life	Scorpio

Blue Phantom Quartz

Properties Blue Phantom Quartz is excellent for enhancing telepathic communication between people on the Earth (each of whom need a crystal), or between Earth and the spiritual realms, assisting you to traverse different dimensions and bring back knowledge from those realms. This is a useful Phantom to support any form of divination as it deepens your attunement, insight and clarity. In making you feel a part of a perfect whole, it helps you to reach out to others with compassion and tolerance.

The Phantom may be formed from Dumortierite (see page 138), in which case Blue Phantom encompasses all the properties of this stalwart crystal.

Beneficial for Ameliorating anger, anxiety, throat, endocrine and metabolic systems, spleen, blood vessels.

Shaped point

Appearance	Chakra	Number	Zodiac sign
Ghostly blue inner point or inclusion	Throat	77	Sagittarius and Aquarius

Black Phantom Quartz

Properties Energetically combining Herkimer and Tibetan Quartz, and carrying an extremely high, sparky vibration, this crystal rapidly opens psychic and inner vision.

Harmonizing the subtle bodies with the physical, Black Phantom Quartz bridges energy gaps along the chakra line.

This rarified stone has a grounded and centred energy that passes into the body and the personal self, bringing about deep healing of the etheric blueprint from which the present physical body devolved, and energizing the meridians.

Beneficial and insightful if it is held by a healer or past-life therapist while working with a client, Black Phantom Quartz accesses the Akashic Record, putting you in touch with ancient Chinese wisdom or highlighting the past-life reasons for dis-ease or karmic lessons being dealt with in the present life.

Beneficial for Energy meridians, cellular memory, auric healing, eating disorders, breaking dependent or co-dependent relationships, centring in one's Self.

Natural double terminations

Appearance	Zodiac sign
Small, clear double-terminated crystals with black inclusions	Capricorn

Amethyst Phantom Quartz

Properties Meditating with Amethyst Phantom facilitates entry into the pre-birth state, accessing the soul plan for the present lifetime, evaluating progress made with spiritual lessons for the current incarnation, and renegotiates or releases these if no longer appropriate. Facilitating travelling to a high vibration, Amethyst Phantom removes implants that operate multidimensionally, healing the etheric or spiritual blueprint and reprogramming cellular memory so that the physical body can raise its vibrations. It has the ability to transport you back into lives where you were priest or priestess to access your spiritual wisdom.

Long point

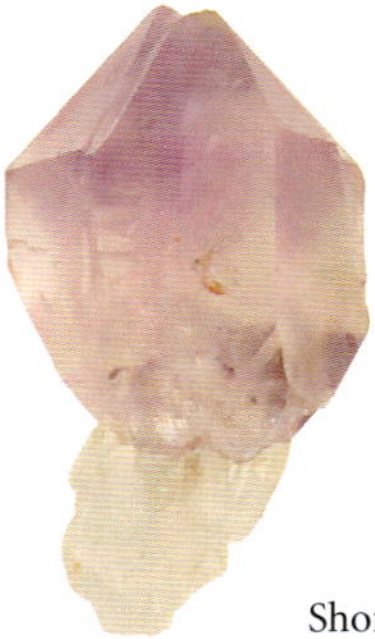

Short point

Appearance	Chakra	Zodiac sign
Ghostly lilac inner point or inclusion	Past life, crown	Pisces

Pink Phantom Quartz

Properties A gentle pacifist, Pink Phantom enhances empathetic communication between friends or lovers (for which two crystals are required), a spirit guide or your higher self as it stimulates telepathy and provides spiritual protection. This Phantom helps you to accept life as it is – and to make changes that bring fulfilment. If two healers are working at a distance, a Pink Phantom provides a strong link between them, especially if a third crystal is with the client.

Beneficial for Restriction, abandonment, betrayal, alienation, the heart, lupus and other auto-immune diseases.

Short point

Natural coated formation

Appearance	Chakra	Zodiac sign
Ghostly pink inner crystal or patch of colour	Heart	Libra

Green Phantom Quartz

Properties Chlorite-included Green Phantom Quartz assists in self-realization and helps you to feel supported. Absorbing negativity and environmental pollutants, it clears a build-up of stagnant energy anywhere in the body or environment. A large Chlorite Phantom placed point down in a lavatory cistern energetically cleanses the whole house. This stone can assist with the removal of energy implants, accessing their source in this or any other lifetime (use under the guidance of an experienced crystal therapist).

Chlorite has strong associations with nature and with Mother Earth and can be used for environmental and Earth cleansing, especially in grids.

Green Phantom Quartz not formed from Chlorite is a wise and powerful healer that accelerates the recovery process. This stone is used for angelic contact and for clarifying clairaudient communication. It can take you back to a time when you had a powerful contact with nature and the nature spirits.

Beneficial for Detoxificaton, cellular memory, convalescence, bi-polar disorder, panic attacks, despair, asthma, ME, chronic fatigue, environmental illness.

Natural point

Appearance	Chakra
Ghostly green inner pyramid or inclusion	Earth, base, solar plexus, heart, third eye, spleen

Indicolite Quartz

Properties Indicolite Quartz has inclusions of Blue Tourmaline, which assists psychic vision and dissolves blocked feelings. Meditating with it puts you in touch with your life purpose and your spiritual helpers. Excellent for stimulating out-of-body experiences and journeying through different realms of consciousness, transports you to a high vibration and offers an overview of your lives and insight into why you have chosen to incarnate again. Ideal for healers, it prevents negativity from sticking and assists in diagnosis and location of the site of dis-ease: the crystal 'jumps' when it reaches the point of greatest disharmony. Place where there is dis-ease or congestion. It is an excellent healer for multidimensional cellular memory.

Beneficial for Sadness, cellular memory, blocked feelings, pulmonary and immune systems, brain, fluid imbalances, kidney, bladder, thymus, thyroid, chronic sore throat, insomnia, night sweats, sinusitis, bacterial infections, throat, larynx, lungs, oesophagus, eyes, burns.

Lightly included

Densely included

Appearance	Chakra	Zodiac sign
Blue threads in Quartz point	Third eye, throat	Taurus, Libra

Lepidocrocite in Quartz or Amethyst

Properties A manifestation empowerment stone taking you beyond time and space to communicate with angelic realms, Lepidocrocite in energizing Quartz or protective Amethyst aligns personal vision with the highest good to manifest dreams and potential. This combination assures you that everything is in perfect order. Excellent for activating spiritual perception, it assists with astral journeying by maintaining contact, via the silver cord, between the physical and etheric bodies. Protecting the soul as it travels, it ensures a smooth return, and enables insights to be brought consciously into the physical body. This combination strengthens awareness of all the bodies, harmonizing the physical, etheric and biomagnetic sheaths. Used with awareness, it takes you forward into the future to see the effects of present actions or to the highest levels of being to meet your true Self. Dissolving false self-image and delusions, it replaces this with true perception. In healing, this combination enhances transfer of Reiki energy or the rebirthing process, facilitates release of blockages, and assists with soul retrieval or house clearing.

Natural point

Appearance	Chakra
Spotted patch or phantom within the crystal	All

Hematite-included Quartz

Properties A useful grounding and protective stone that is strongly yang, Hematite has an extremely beneficial effect on blood and prevents negative energies from entering the subtle bodies. It assists the soul in returning to the body after spiritual journeying. Hematite-included Quartz is an excellent energizer that invigorates, cheers and rejuvenates. Particularly useful when you feel without hope, it restores optimism and faith in the future. Strengthening and focusing the mind and improving concentration, Hematite-included Quartz supports problem-solving and technical matters such as mathematics.

This stone is helpful for timid women who need to make their presence felt – keep one in your pocket or wear as jewellery. It can also be used to attract kind and loving relationships or to revitalize an existing relationship.

Beneficial for Balancing yin-yang, circulation, production of red blood cells, energizing the blood, kidneys, tissue regeneration, cramps, anxiety, insomnia.

Polished

Appearance
May appear as a phantom, spot or red patch

Quartz with Mica

Properties A combination of energizing Quartz and Mica, a mystical stone that spreads energy out in several layers at once and assists in getting to the bottom of things, this ancient shamanic stone heightens intuition and the ability to act on this in a practical manner. If you wish to sharpen your dreamwork, perception or progression along the spiritual path, Quartz with Mica assists by heightening connection to your spiritual Self, facilitating transmutation and connection to unconditional love and enhancing ability to distinguish true intuition from instincts and compulsions of the subconscious mind or unconscious longings of the emotional self.

Quartz with Mica heightens the energetic response to acupuncture and acupressure. Passing Quartz with Mica around the body identifies and seals the site of energy leakage and transmutes negative energy held in the chakras or aura. It is excellent for multidimensional cellular memory healing.

'Soulmate' with Mica base

Beneficial for Rebirthing, cellular memory, eating disorders, motor skills, macular degeneration.

Appearance	Chakra	Number	Zodiac sign
Mica flakes included in or protruding from Quartz	Third eye, crown, aligns all	3	Cancer

Quartz on Sphalerite

Properties A powerful energy cleanser that removes mental overload and lightens dark moods, Quartz on Sphalerite has been described as a 'settling out' stone that ameliorates alienation and isolation, creating balance. Amplifying insight when stroked in a meditative state, it invokes light and facilitates journeying. The Sphalerite component helps you to recognize deceit and to ascertain whether channelled or other information is 'truth' or deception. This stone aligns the etheric bodies with the physical so that information is more readily available. Sphalerite anchors those for whom the Earth is not their natural home into incarnation, making them feel more comfortable. It overcomes homesickness wherever this occurs.

Balancing male and female energies within the body and personality, Quartz on Sphalerite helps with gender alignment, especially where the soul inhabits a different sexual body from the last incarnation. It is an excellent protective stone for anyone who works in the public eye.

Beneficial for Environmental disease, eyes, nervous system.

Natural formation

Appearance	Chakra
Drusy Quartz on metallic grey matrix	Base

Ajoite

Properties An extremely high-vibration and rare stone, as the original South African mine has flooded, Ajoite wraps the soul in universal love. If your vibrations are in harmony with this stone it brings about a profound spiritual revelation and serenity. A purifier for the emotional body and instilling infinite peace, Ajoite creates emotional and environmental calm, gently drawing out and transmuting toxic emotions and old grief. Worn over the thymus, it dissipates stress from the physical body and, harmonizing the etheric blueprint with the physical body, attunes to a state of perfect health. Ajoite resolves conflict by highlighting the need for forgiveness and compassion that encompasses yourself and others.

Ajoite draws karmic wounds or implants out of the body no matter at what level or from which timeframe they originate, and gently heals the resulting space with unconditional love, reframing cellular memory.

Beneficial for Cellular memory, releasing toxic emotions, forgiveness, compassion, serenity, stress, regenerating cellular structures.

Raw

Appearance	Chakra	Number	Zodiac sign
Translucent phantom or combination with other minerals	Third eye, crown, links heart and throat	6	Virgo

Molybdenite in Quartz

Properties Combining the strongly energizing, cleansing and amplifying properties of Quartz with Molybdenite (see page 100), this stone helps you to tap into subconscious knowledge and opens spiritual insight whilst at the same time affording protection.

Molybdenite in Quartz is extremely beneficial for group working and for harmonizing the energies and auras of two or more people. This is especially so when working with crystals and much insight can be gained this way. It assists in knowing that you are not alone, and is said to bring light into darkness.

This combination effectively removes mental blockages and outgrown baggage from one's life and is extremely useful for gaining insight from your dreams. Place under a pillow to stimulate lucid dreaming.

Natural formation

Appearance
Small metallic patches in opaque white matrix

Epidote in Quartz

Properties Combining the highly energizing properties of Quartz with Epidote (see page 119), this hopeful stone provides rejuvenation and the courage to bounce back after enormous setbacks, adding a new impetus to soul growth. The Quartz amplifies the emotional energy purification afforded by Epidote and may create a cathartic reaction best handled by an experienced therapist as other crystals may be required to soften the effect. It is extremely useful if you easily fall victim to other people's manipulative interventions in your life. Programme it and keep it in your pocket or beside your bed for maximum effect.

Beneficial for Convalescence, grief, bruises, sprains, pain.

Natural formation

Appearance	Chakra
Dark streaks in Quartz	Higher heart

Ocean Orbicular Jasper (The Atlantis Stone)

Properties Discovered in Madagascar at the millennium, Ocean Jasper is mined at low tide and, as such, is said to be connected to Atlantis and to hold mystic knowledge within it. Known as 'the supreme nurturer', Jasper holds the generic properties of sustenance, support and unification. Grounding energy into the body, it is excellent for aligning the chakras, the subtle bodies and the meridians and is a useful support during shamanic journeying. It provides protection from negative energies of all kinds.

Ocean Jasper provides a link between the moon and the sun and their associated zodiac signs of Cancer and Leo, and unites past and present. It brings together the underlying emotional self and the outer façade of personality, creating a wholeness. Meditating with this stone takes you back into the past to reclaim your wisdom or to reframe and transmute misuse of spiritual power at that time. The swirling patterns symbolize the interconnectedness of all things, supporting service to humankind. A stone of renewal and strength, Ocean Jasper assists in loving yourself and others, being more empathetic to their emotional and mental needs while remaining objective and detached.

Reminding us that nature is cyclical, rhythmical and fluid, Ocean Jasper assists in coping with necessary change. With its gentle nurturing energy, Ocean Jasper brings to the surface long hidden unresolved emotional issues and helps you to face the future positively, accepting responsibility for yourself. Its circular markings resonate with circular breathing, which it facilitates, and anything that cycles and circulates. It is an excellent lymph-drainage stimulator.

This stone is said to eliminate the toxins that cause body odour. If Drusy Quartz is within the stone, it focuses and intensifies healing intention and recuperation. The Green Jasper component heals and releases dis-ease and obsession, balancing parts of your life that have become all-important to the detriment of others.

Beneficial for Patience, detoxifying, stress, immune system, lymph, circulation, debilitated internal organs, female reproductive system, PMS, digestion, tumours, gum infections, eczema, cysts, colds, hallucinations, insomnia, toxicity, inflammation, skin disorders, bloating, upper torso, digestive tract, purifying organs.

Appearance	Chakra	Number	Zodiac sign
Whorls, contour lines and bands of opaque stone, interspersed with druse	Heart, solar plexus	6	Cancer, Leo

Raw, sliced and polished

Tumbled

Leopardskin Jasper (Jaguar Stone)

Properties Leopardskin Jasper is said to be redressing the balance between light and dark, recognizing the value of dark as a complement to light rather than its enemy. It is a shape-shifter's stone that passes between the worlds.

Extremely helpful in assisting fulfilling karmic agreements or soul contracts made before incarnating; if those contracts are no longer appropriate this stone assists you to rescind or renegotiate the terms and intent. Leopardskin Jasper shuts off outer vision, focusing perception, and insists you listen to your own inner voice. Conversely, by mirroring the outside world back to you, Leopardskin Jasper clears ingrained assumptions and teaches you to see what *is*, assessing your situation more clearly.

This stone reduces insecurities, heals the emotional body and strengthens sense of individuality. If you need balance between passivity and activity, spirituality and emotion, Leopardskin Jasper is the perfect tool. Delineating your life path, it provides protection while encouraging you to meet your challenges and fulfil your goals. Fortifying your body's natural resistance, Leopardskin Jasper assists in maintaining health.

This stone engenders respect for native peoples and their innate wisdom and healing ways, and opens and maintains a connection between humankind and the animal world, bringing about environmental harmony.

Beneficial for Cellular memory, guilt, fear, insomnia, emotional stress, tissue regeneration, protection, digestive processes, 12-strand DNA healing, excretion, abdominal pain, skin diseases, kidney or gallstones.

Tumbled stones

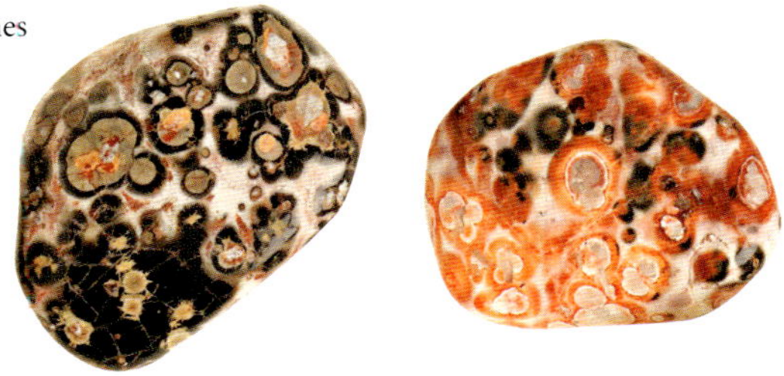

Appearance	Chakra	Number
Opaque leopard-like markings	Base, heart, crown	8

Rainforest Jasper

Properties Inhaling the aroma of Rainforest Jasper immediately connects you to nature. A natural healer, especially for cellular memory, it draws your attention to the action of plants and reactivates herbal-healing knowledge from the far past. It passes on knowledge, especially through the female line, accessing ancestral matriarchs to reconnect to the family myths by which they lived. If you are lost at a soul level, this stone takes you back to your roots to re-anchor yourself and reassess your situation objectively.

Rainforest encourages emotional balance and, with its ability to pause the mind, this is a 'stone of being' that allows you to move effortlessly back into balance, and to accept yourself as you are without needing to change. Rainforest Jasper balances humidity, creating conditions that are neither too damp nor excessively dry.

Beneficial for Self-respect, objectivity, clarity, imagination, creativity, cellular memory, flu, colds, susceptibility to damp, viral infections, fluid imbalances.

Raw

Appearance	Chakra
Mossy opaque stone with an earthy smell	Earth, base and spleen

Tree Agate

Properties Strongly grounded and calming, Tree Agate instils a feeling of safety in the most challenging of situations, offering protection against negativity. Imparting strength, it helps face unpleasant circumstances with fortitude and equanimity, and to find the gift in their heart. This stone helps you to have a positive ego and unshakeable self-esteem. A useful Earth healer, Tree Agate is an excellent stone for plants and trees of all kinds, and can be gridded around a growing area. This stone assists in making a powerful connection to the nurturing energy of nature and nature spirits, restoring and reviving vitality and perseverance, and enhancing rapport with living things.

If your immune system is weak and you are susceptible to infection, tape Tree Agate over your thymus and leave in place overnight.

Beneficial for Security, immune system, bacterial infections.

Raw

Tumbled

Appearance	Chakra
Opaque white stone flecked with green	Higher heart

Botswana and Grey-banded Agate

Properties These Banded Agates share properties. Placed on the third eye, Banded Agate cuts mental cords to a guru, partner or parent who capitalizes on a past connection to retain manipulative control in the present. Excellent for replenishing energy lost in such situations, it draws on a higher life force and protects the aura. It is an excellent healer for reprogramming cellular memory, especially old mortification of flesh, emotions or spirit.

Gridded around a house, it prevents out-of-body visitations. Its bands take you travelling into other realities, different streams of consciousness, or other lives, and are extremely effective for multidimensional healing and soul work.

Programme it to protect you and your family and to encourage supportive, objective and non-smothering love.

Banded Agate stimulates the crown chakra, bringing celestial and Earth energy into the auric field and harmonizing the physical body with the subtle bodies, balancing body, mind, emotions and spirit, removing dualities and conflicts and maintaining well-being. Traditionally used to overcome physical, emotional and mental poisoning, and useful for people who are easily hurt, it teaches you to look to solutions rather than problems. Giving the broader picture, it explores unknown territory while paying appropriate attention to detail. Botswana Agate is excellent for anyone connected with fire or smoke, especially smokers and those who want to quit. It is said that Banded Agate repels spiders. If you experience giddiness remove at once.

Beneficial for Artistic expression, cellular memory, depression, releasing emotional repression, detoxification, sensuality, multidimensional healing, sexuality, fertility, the brain, assimilating oxygen, chest, circulatory and nervous systems, skin.

Botswana Agate

Grey-banded Agate

Appearance	Chakra	Number	Zodiac sign
Closely banded opaque stone (Botswana is pinker than Grey-banded)	Crown	3	Scorpio

Hematoid Calcite

Properties Infusing the stabilizing and staying power of Hematite (see page 68) with the protective and purifying energies of Calcite, Hematoid Calcite is an excellent stone if you experience an influx of energy that needs grounding and assimilating. Simply hold it or place over the base chakra for five or ten minutes or until the energy stabilizes. Grid around a room or carry one whenever you are in a strong energy field, particularly if the energies clash, as it will quickly cleanse and harmonize the environment around you.

Hematoid Calcite is a supportive stone for the memory, so if you lose things, or cannot remember birthdays or names, this is the stone for you.

Beneficial for Memory, blood cleansing and oxygenation, stress.

Raw

Appearance	Chakra
Large squares or planes of reddish-yellow opaque crystal	Higher crown, solar plexus, base

Cobalto-calcite (Cobaltite)

Properties Calcite is a powerful amplifier and cleanser of energy that speeds development and facilitates opening higher awareness and promotes emotional intelligence. Although in the past connected to goblins, crystal healers see Cobalto-calcite as symbolizing unconditional love and forgiveness. This stone is excellent for emotional healing; it soothes intense feelings, assisting you to love yourself and others, and to feel good about your life. This beautiful crystal harmonizes intellect and emotion and transfers ideas into action. A stone of self-discovery connecting heart with mind, gentle Cobalto-calcite facilitates finding your innate talents and life purpose. It is extremely supportive for those who carry pain for other people or the planet, and for those who have given up hope. Place Cobalto-calcite on a photograph for distance healing and programme it to send pink light to support someone in becoming all that they might be, or to overcome an emotional block.

Beneficial for Emotional maturation, nurturing, scars, broken heart, loneliness, grief.

Raw on matrix

Appearance	Chakra	Number	Zodiac sign
Small clear pink crystals on a matrix	Heart	8	Cancer

Icicle Calcite

Properties A mix of orange and white Calcite, Icicle Calcite is a guidance crystal that increases the ability to see things in a new way and fires your creativity. Releasing fear, it assists in stepping forward into the future to confidently live out your purpose.

As with all Calcite, Icicle Calcite is a powerful amplifier of energy with strong purifying and cleansing properties that quickly remove stagnant energies and restore vitality. The white portion of Icicle Calcite can be used like a wand to pull multidimensional dis-ease, disharmony or blockages from the physical or subtle bodies and, once the crystal has been cleansed, the resulting 'hole' can be repaired and re-energized with the orange portion. It works extremely well for past-life dis-ease.

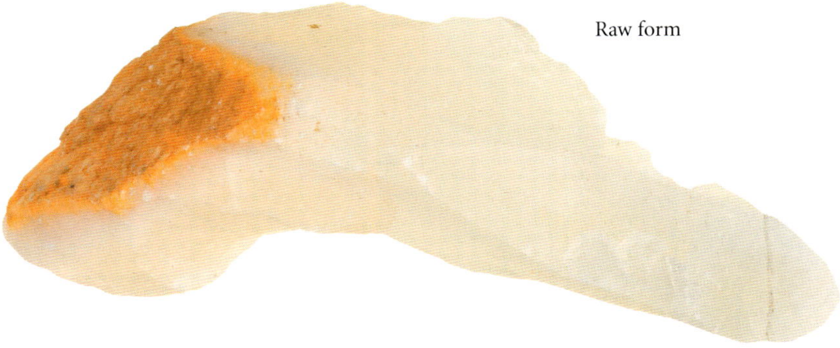

Raw form

Appearance	Chakra
Long finger-like opaque two-colour crystal	Solar plexus, third eye, clears all

Heulandite

Properties Heulandite is an excellent stone if you want to move on. Taking you back into the past to release negative emotions, it assists in recovering from loss and in changing ingrained habits or behaviours, especially those held at a cellular level, replacing these with openness to new ways and opening exciting possibilities. Highly decorative, it can be programmed and left in your environment to bring about quietly the changes you seek.

This stone also takes you into the past beneficially, to regain ancient knowledge and skills from Lemuria and Atlantis and to access your own past lives. It assists in traversing interdimensional spaces and facilitates reading and understanding the Akashic Record.

Beneficial for Cellular memory, mobility, weight reduction, growths, lower limbs, blood flow, kidneys, liver.

Raw form

Appearance	Chakra	Number	Zodiac sign
Crystalline to vitreous opaque pearly crystals on a matrix	Solar plexus, soma	9	Sagittarius

Peach Selenite

Properties A stone of emotional transformation carrying all the purity and highly spiritual energetic properties of Selenite, Peach Selenite is a powerful cleanser and healer and is the perfect accompaniment for those who are immersed in old trauma and who need to review their lives, particularly if circumstances have necessitated a trip into the underworld. Drawing out issues of abandonment, rejection, alienation and betrayal, no matter when these occurred, nurturing Peach Selenite transmutes the energy into healing, forgiveness and acceptance. This stone is useful for those who unconsciously prefer to stay with the discomfort of a condition rather than face the challenge of getting well and understanding the psychosomatic cause.

Symbolizing the transmuting fires of the planet Pluto and the earthy wisdom of his wife Persephone, Peach Selenite is the perfect accompaniment for an evolutionary jump into self-awareness and new life. This is a stone that affords deep insight into the cycles of birth, death and rebirth and which opens the priestess in every woman. It is perfect for thanksgiving moon rituals at times of transition such as puberty or childbirth.

Raw

Appearance	Chakra	Zodiac sign	Planet
Finely ribbed opaque stone	All, especially solar plexus and sacral	Cancer	Pluto

Selenite Phantom

Properties A Selenite Phantom acts in a similar manner to other phantoms to strip away all that has been overlaid on the soul core, but can assist when working at the highest spiritual vibration to connect to the true spiritual Self and its overall evolutionary purpose. Carrying purity and the highly spiritual energetic properties of Selenite, a nurturing stone that instils clarity of mind and protects against being overwhelmed mentally or physically, the Phantom clears mental and spiritual confusion and removes karmic entanglements. The insights gained can be grounded and earthed into the physical body with the wider end of the Phantom. If pointed, Selenite Phantom cuts through karmic debris, especially when used as a wand to draw it off and reprogramme cellular memory, and dissolve emotional dis-ease. The crystal then acts as a symbol of rebirth and new life.

Beneficial for Cellular memory, spinal column alignment, joint flexibility, neutralizing mercury toxicity.

Natural point

Appearance	Chakra	Zodiac sign
Solid crystal within clear Selenite	All	Cancer

Black Kyanite

Properties A potent tool for fully incarnating into Earth life and for moving into the between-life state to access the current lifeplan, and other lives if necessary, Black Kyanite can view the karma you are currently creating by showing in a future life the results of choices made now, and can assist in foreseeing the outcome of a plan. A particularly powerful stone for psychological and auric cleansing that never needs cleansing. Used like a wand, the striations rapidly move negativity out of the subtle bodies, aligning and grounding the chakras, and draw dis-ease and stagnant energy from the physical body, replenishing it with positive energy and reprogrammed cellular memory. With strong links to the Earth, Black Kyanite supports Earth healing, environmentalism and connects with those who are assisting the evolution of the planet. It is said to keep cells connected to the overall divine blueprint to maintain health.

Beneficial for Environmental detoxification, mental cleansing, urogenital and reproductive system, muscles, adrenals, throat, parathyroid.

Raw

Appearance	Chakra
Striated opaque stone	Aligns and grounds all

Crystalline Kyanite

Properties This lively stone has a very light and fast vibration that never needs cleansing and quickly activates the higher chakras and the mind, linking you to your life path and true vocation. As with all Kyanite, Crystalline Kyanite is excellent for moving rapidly into deep meditation and opening metaphysical gifts, making multidimensional connections of all kinds.

This is a useful stone to smooth the way for lasting relationships, for which it needs two stones – one in the possession of each person. The stones can be programmed to enhance appropriate telepathic and intuitive communication between the two people concerned and to bring harmony and unconditional love to the partnership. As this stone could be used for psychic spying, it must be used with integrity of purpose or it will rebound on the wearer.

Beneficial for Ovarian or ovulation pain.

Polished

Appearance	Chakra	Number
Lightly striated clear blue crystal	Higher crown, aligns all	2

Oregon Opal

Properties A highly spiritual stone that carries the opaline vibration of cosmic consciousness and facilitates moving between dimensions, Oregon Opal is a reflective stone that assists in past-life exploration, showing where that you put out in one life has returned in another, and is an extremely effective tool for releasing old grief, trauma and disappointment from the present or any other life.

This stone searches out lies, both those from other people and those arising from our own self-deceptions and delusions. Clearing the emotional body, it amplifies the entire range of positive emotions and can act as an emotional stabilizer, being more gentle in its effect than pure Opal.

Beneficial for Purification, excess mucus, fever, eyes.

Raw

Appearance	Chakra
Opaline stone often in a matrix	Throat, solar plexus, heart

Girasol (Blue Opal)

Properties An excellent visioning stone that reveals solutions to current difficulties especially where these are created by something that could not be spoken about in the past, or was suppressed through lack of confidence. Girasol enhances connections between souls and shows how these can be beneficial in the present life.

Girasol is extremely useful when past-life experiences or injuries are affecting the present life. These can be healed through the etheric blueprint as Girasol dissolves the 'scars', allowing the physical body to release the condition and cellular memory to heal.

An emotional comforter that realigns you to your spiritual purpose, Girasol enhances all communications. Pinpointing your hidden feelings and the psychic impressions you may inadvertently pick up, it helps you to know the deeper causes of discontent, strengthens your boundaries and teaches you how to satisfy your emotional needs.

An excellent stone for stimulating creativity, Girasol creates a quiet space in which to work and meditate.

Beneficial for Panic, phobias, creativity, cellular memory, assimilation of iron, vision, fatigue, metabolism, hair loss, lymph nodes.

Polished

Appearance	Chakra	Number	Zodiac sign
May be clear and jelly-like, or opaque	Third eye	3, 9	Taurus

Andean Blue Opal

Properties Carrying the refined spiritual vibration of Opal and its link to love and passion and an ability to strengthen the will to live, Andean Blue Opal promotes acting for the highest good and is excellent for stimulating communication from the heart as it smoothes the auric field, enhancing connection and communication with others. It is particularly useful for healing old emotional wounds, from this life or another, and for finding the inner serenity to carry you through troubled times or stress. An excellent journeying stone, Andean Opal creates a relaxed, receptive state and can induce mild hypnotic trance, enhancing divination and clairvoyance.

Increasing awareness of the need for healing the Earth, this is a useful tool for facilitating that healing and for those who manifest and transmute the changing vibration through their own physical or subtle body.

Beneficial for 'Right action', cellular memory, Parkinson's, water retention, muscular swelling, heart, lungs, thymus.

Cut and polished

Appearance	Chakra	Number	Zodiac sign
Opaque, slightly iridescent blue stone	Throat, heart, higher heart (thymus), third eye	2	Aries, Virgo

Rainbow Moonstone

Properties A form of Moonstone, a lunar-orientated stone of new beginnings that opens intuition and calms emotions, Rainbow Moonstone houses a spiritual being that carries the vibration of cosmic light and offers spiritual healing for the whole of humanity. As with Moonstone, this stone is powerfully attuned to the cycles and phases of the moon and may need to be removed at full moon as it heightens psychic sensitivity at that time. Rainbow Moonstone reminds you that you are part of an ongoing, ever unfolding cycle and links you into your overall live plan as well as the current life plan. It helps you to see the unseen, to intuitively read symbols and synchronicities, and open to spiritual gifts.

If you are highly sensitive, Rainbow Moonstone may leave you open to psychic or emotional overwhelm from external sources and may need to be removed when in a crowd, although it can help with insight in the appropriate circumstances.

Beneficial for Female reproductive organs and dis-eases, fluid retention, insomnia, sleepwalking, degenerative conditions, internal organs, eyes, arteries and veins.

Polished

Tumbled

Appearance	Chakra	Number	Zodiac sign
Opaque to crystalline stone with iridescent rainbows	All	77	Cancer

Bornite

Properties Fostering concern about all beings on the planet, advocating social justice and equality for all, Bornite teaches you how to negotiate obstacles with the least stress and encourages you to find happiness in the present moment. Opening psychic abilities and enhancing inner knowing, it teaches trust in the intuitive process. Assisting with visualization and creating your own reality, Bornite can be programmed to send or receive healing from a distance – in which case it should be carried or worn over the thymus (preferably set in silver).

Bornite is an excellent tool during any kind of rebirthing work or traumatic situation. Integrating mind, body, emotions and soul, it filters out what is no longer relevant. An excellent protection against negativity, which it transmutes, Bornite assists in identifying the source of detrimental thoughts so that they can be eliminated.

Note that Bornite is a toxic stone and should be worn or used only in tumbled form, especially for preparing elixirs.

Beneficial for Fairness, peace, regeneration, cellular memory, cellular structures, metabolic imbalances, dissolving calcified deposits, over-acidity, assimilation of potassium, swelling.

Tumbled

Appearance	Chakra	Number	Zodiac sign
Opaque, metallic, tarnishes to iridescent	Third eye, crown, activates and synthesizes all	2, 4	Cancer

Bornite on Silver

Properties Silver is an energizing and stabilizing metal that strengthens the qualities of the stone to which it is attached and focuses the energy appropriately. As silver is a feminine, moon-attuned metal, it can act as a reflective mirror for mystic visions, scrying or inspiration, heightening perception and intuition. Bornite on Silver reinforces the silver cord that connects the astral body to the physical, ensuring safe return whenever and wherever you journey, keep it close to you for protection. It is particularly useful for accessing and reframing the cause of third-eye blockages, especially where these have been deliberately proscribed in the past, and facilitates cellular memory reprogramming.

Bornite on Silver enhances mothering and the nurturing process, and platonic or romantic love.

Raw

Appearance	Chakra
Metallic shimmering stone	Third eye

Specular Hematite

Properties Sparking silver-blue light enlivens the deep grey of ethereal Specular Hematite. Carrying the protective and grounding properties of Hematite, it earths high-frequency spiritual energies into everyday reality and shifts the physical vibration of the subtle and gross physical bodies so that they can more effectively receive and assimilate those energies. This stone assists in manifesting your own unique spirit here on Earth, and in identifying where your particular talents can best be used.

Specular Hematite counteracts electromagnetic energies and is a useful stone to place by a computer as it harmonizes the interaction between the computer and the physical body, raising the vibrations of both.

Beneficial for Haemoglobin, anaemia, blood disorders, electromagnetic stress.

Raw

Appearance	Chakra	Zodiac sign
Dark and sparkling like a night sky	Earth and crown	Aquarius

Conichalcite

Properties Conichalcite is a form of copper and as such is a powerful energy conduit. It provides a shield against everyday concerns and stimulates intuition. Copper has been dedicated to the goddess Venus for over six thousand years and this stone assists you to bring heart and mind together, creating personal empowerment and an inner strength that is tempered and flexible enough to accommodate change.

A stone of communication, Conichalcite assists in quietening the mind ready for meditation, leaving behind concerns about the world, and opening the way for limitless possibilities to manifest. This stone also facilitates communication with the plant and nature kingdom.

Beneficial for Detoxification, mucus, kidneys, bladder, psoriasis, herpes.

Deposition on matrix

Crystals on matrix

Appearance	Chakra	Number	Zodiac sign	Planet
Vitreous mass or translucent crystal	Heart, third eye, solar plexus	3	Pisces	Venus

Limonite

Properties The generic name for iron oxide and a colourant in several stones to which it adds properties (Bushman Cascade Quartz, see page 25, and Red and Yellow Phantom Quartz, see pages 58 and 60), Limonite is a grounding and protective stone that stabilizes your life and stimulates your inner strength, particularly when faced with extreme conditions. Affording the physical body protection during metaphysical activities, Limonite guards against mental influence or psychic attack and psychic overwhelm. This stone is a powerful mental facilitator, sharpening the mind and ameliorating confusion. It enhances telepathy and facilitates inner-child healing with the support of other stones. Traditionally used as a treatment for dehydration, Limonite is also excellent for removing yourself from the mire, whatever form that may take, and promoting objectivity. It facilitates standing firm without needing to fight back and favourably assists legal situations. The stone restores youthful properties.

Beneficial for Dehydration, cleansing, endurance, efficiency, musculoskeletal system, iron and calcium assimilation, jaundice, fevers, liver, digestion.

Raw

Appearance	Chakra	Number	Zodiac sign	Planet
Glassy dense mass, metallic or dull and rusty, may be occluded	Sacral, base, earth	7	Virgo	Mars

Rutile

Properties Rutile is often included within other crystals to which it imparts an ethereal vibration that enhances out-of-body journeying, psychic protection and angelic contact. A powerful cleansing agent, it purifies the biomagnetic sheath, bringing it into balance with the physical body. Going directly to the root of a problem, Rutile heals psychosomatic dis-ease, pinpoints karmic causes of chronic illness and reprogrammes cellular memory. It stabilizes relationships, creating emotional fidelity to underpin partnership.

The reddish-brown colour of Rutile is useful in counteracting sexual problems, bringing the reasons for those conditions into conscious awareness to be reframed and released. (Place the crystal a hand's breadth below the navel before asking to see the cause. Guidance from a qualified therapist assists the process.)

Beneficial for Lactation, cellular memory, elasticity of blood vessels, cell regeneration, bronchitis, premature ejaculation, impotence, frigidity, inorgasmia.

Sliced rutilated Quartz with Rutile crystals

Appearance	Chakra	Number	Zodiac sign
Metallic crystalline, often fine included needles	Sacral	4	Taurus, Gemini

Bronzite

Properties Bronzite is a protective, grounding crystal that is helpful in discordant situations where you feel powerless and in the grip of events beyond your control, as it restores harmony and self-assertion without invoking wilfulness or aggression.

This stone is said to be a 'stone of courtesy' that strengthens non-judgemental discernment, pinpoints your most important choices and promotes decisive action. Enhancing your self-esteem, it allows you simply to 'be', entering a dynamic state of non-action, non-doing.

Bronzite is marketed as being particularly effective against curses. However, traditionally, iron-bearing crystals such as Bronzite return ill-wishing, curses or spells back to the source magnified three times over. This perpetuates the curse as it bounces backward and forward, becoming stronger each time. It may be sensible to use a crystal such as Black Tourmaline, which absorbs and neutralizes the curse once and for all.

Beneficial for Masculine energy, over-alkalinity, assimilation of iron.

Tumbled stones

Appearance	Chakra	Number	Zodiac sign
Opaque, lustrous flecked stone	Activates and synthesizes all	1	Leo

Chalcopyrite

Properties Meaning 'sparks when struck', Chalcopyrite is said to put you through 'the fires of truth'. An excellent aid to achieving the state of 'no mind' required for deep meditation and contemplation of the perfection of the universe, it assists in assimilating spiritual knowledge, linking you to ancient civilizations or the cause of present-life difficulties or dis-eases. Chalcopyrite supports accurate perception and logical thought while listening to your inner voice.

A powerful energy conduit, Chalcopyrite supports during Tai Chi and is excellent for heightening acupuncture or acupressure as it dissolves energy blockages and enhances the movement of *Qi* around the body, stabilizing cell energy as higher frequencies are integrated. This stone is reported to locate lost objects and itself disappears and reappears into different realities. Attracting abundance, it shows you that prosperity is a state of mind.

Beneficial for Self-esteem, self-knowledge, inner security, insight, cellular memory, energy blockages, hair growth, thread veins, brain disorders, excretory organs, tumours, infectious diseases, RNA/DNA, arthritis, bronchitis, inflammation, fever.

Tumbled

Appearance	Chakra	Number	Zodiac sign
Opaque brassy yellow crystal that tarnishes to many colours	Crown	9	Capricorn

Molybdenite

Properties Known as the dreamer's stone, Molybdenite integrates your everyday self with your higher self and is a useful tool for facing and accepting your shadow and perfecting your character. If you need an insightful or healing dream, place programmed Molybdenite under your pillow. This powerful stone also assists healers in their work and is reputed to facilitate intergalactic contact.

Molybdenite operates exceptionally well at a mental level and through the subtle energy bodies, which it repairs and replenishes. Keeping the stone in your energy field allows for continual recharging and rebalancing as it has a strong electrical charge – sensitive people may need to remove it periodically. Molybdenite is useful for eliminating mercury toxicity from the body, and for harmonizing mercury fillings to a more beneficial vibration.

Beneficial for Jaw pain, teeth, circulation, oxygenation, immune system.

Molybdenite on a Quartz matrix

Appearance	Chakra	Number	Zodiac sign
Metallic, dense crystal, feels greasy to the touch	Third eye, base	7	Scorpio

Stibnite

Properties Stibnite carries the energy of wolf, facilitating journeying with this shamanic power animal. In meditation, Stibnite forms an energetic shield around the physical body and is an excellent stone for separating out the pure from the dross, and for releasing entity possession or negative energy. This stone works brilliantly to help you to see the gold in your own centre, and to find the gift in difficult experiences.

Assisting in eliminating 'tentacles' from clingy present or previous relationships that penetrate the auric or physical bodies, especially after physical separation, it can be helpful in tie-cutting rituals and past-life releases. Stibnite is particularly useful in situations where you find it difficult to say no to a former partner – although, having tie-cut, when you next hold Stibnite it may evoke a situation that tests out that the cutting is complete.

Beneficial for Astral travel, cellular memory, rigidity, oesophagus, stomach.

Natural wands

Appearance	Chakra	Number	Zodiac sign
Metallic, needle-like fans and blades that tarnish	Base, sacral, soma, solar plexus	8	Scorpio, Capricorn

Septarian

Properties With a nourishing and calming energy, Septarian is an excellent support for self-nurturing, caring about others and for taking care of the Earth – the grey concretions connecting to devic energy.

Bringing together the energy-cleansing and amplifying qualities of Calcite, Earth-healing and grounding properites of Aragonite and the nurturing and stabilizing energies of Chalcedony, this joyous stone supports you while you incubate ideas and assists in bringing them to fruition, inculcating patience, tolerance and endurance. Conversely, if you are someone who always has ideas but never puts them into practice, it will ground your creativity.

The ideal NLP stone, Septarian assists in repatterning and reprogramming, and directs the practitioner to the most appropriate tools. At a spiritual level, Septarian harmonizes emotions and intellect with the higher mind.

Septarian is a useful support during public speaking as it assists in making each individual within an audience feel that they are being personally addressed. Keep a piece with you and you will hold your audience in the palm of your hand.

Septarian also enhances your ability to communicate within a group. This stone is reported to have been used to focus the healing vibrations within drumming and chanting circles.

This stone enhances the cohesiveness of any spiritual group, and healers can use it for diagnosis and insight into the cause of dis-ease.

Septarian is extremely helpful in focusing the body's own healing ability.

Beneficial for Seasonal affective disorder, self-healing, cellular memory, metabolism, growths, intestines, kidneys, blood, skin disorders, heart, geopathic stress.

Appearance	Chakra	Number	Zodiac sign
Nodules filled with fissures lined with transparent crystals or gritty stone	Base; synthesizes heart, throat and third eye	66, 3	Taurus, Sagittarius

Polished egg, natural centre

Nuummite

Properties Said to be the oldest mineral on Earth, Nuummite is the sorcerer's stone. Scintillating flashes assist in seeing beyond the outer façade, and create an inner landscape to be traversed. A protective stone, strengthening the auric shield and effective against pollutants and sorcery, Nuummite helps you to travel with stealth and sureness. It shields from sight and safeguards your car. This powerful stone needs to be used respectfully, with right intention, or it could rebound. Nuummite assists in recognizing past-life contacts and highlights karmic debts stemming from misuse of power. Placed on the soma chakra it draws karmic debris out of the physical and emotional bodies. With its strong electromagnetic field, Nuummite quickly restores energy and power that has been depleted by karmic debts or other causes, and clears blockages including those that are self-imposed, reprogramming cellular memory. Severing entanglements that stem from past manipulation or incantations, Nuummite removes difficulties that arise from another person's misguided protection of you, then reconnects your true Self. It allows you to reprogramme thoughts and to be responsible for your own protection. Nuummite teaches respect and honour, fulfilling obligations and promises that are relevant to life today, encouraging serendipitous synchronicity. This stone aligns the aura with the physical body, and removes mental implants from an extraterrestrial or magical source.

Beneficial for Change, intuition, insomnia, stress, degenerative disease, brain, tissue regeneration, strengthening triple burner meridian, Parkinson's disease, headache, insulin regulation, eyes, kidneys, nerves.

Sliced and polished

Appearance	Chakra	Number	Zodiac sign
Opaque, deep black with scintillating flashes	Past life, soma, opens and integrates all	3	Sagittarius

Novaculite

Properties Traditionally used as a whetstone and arrowhead, Novaculite hones the spirit and the psyche and creates an intense one-pointed strongly focused energy beam. This stone has an extremely light and high energy that facilitates angelic contact and multidimensional journeying. An excellent conductor of electromagnetic energy, Novaculite is beneficial for the etheric body and for making necessary amendments to clear dis-ease out of the etheric blueprint. It is helpful in finding the gift in any situation, no matter how dire it may seem.

The ultimate cord-cutting tool, Novaculite glides through blockages and problems, and through the ties that etherically link people together. Used at the chakras, it cuts these cords and heals the site. Used on the etheric body, Novaculite performs psychic surgery – although care must be taken as the stone has a razor-sharp edge and this operation should be carried out by a qualified healer.

Because of its very fine texture, Novaculite has the ability to bring structure and elasticity to the physical body, particularly the skin, or to the environment around you. An extremely placid and calming stone, it is beneficial for those who are in the depths of despair or the grip of an obsession. Helpful to anyone who sells services to others, it brings buyer and seller together, enhancing one's own personal magnetism. It is reported that this stone boosts interstellar contact and assists in deciphering ancient languages. Novaculite works well with Nuummite.

Beneficial for Obtaining a new perspective, cellular memory, depression, obsessive disorders, warts, moles, chills, cellular structure, healthy skin.

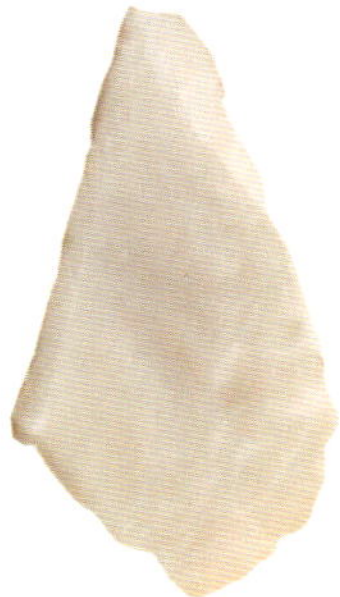

Raw flake

Appearance	Chakra	Number	Zodiac sign
Lustrous, translucent to opaque, waxy fine-textured stone	Crown and higher crown, opens, energizes and aligns all	5	Scorpio

Datolite

Properties Datolite assists in seeing and accepting the transience of all things, ensuring that you know that 'this too will pass' and, therefore, it is a useful stone to keep with you during violent upheaval or tumultuous change. A problem-solving stone that improves study skills, its attributes include clarity of thought and enhanced concentration, leading to an ability to remember fine detail where appropriate and teaching how to discard the rest. It enhances mature thought and the flow of ideas.

When meditated with, Datolite facilitates the retrieval of information encoded in the subtle DNA, retrieving ancestral patterns and events, and in the soul and far memory. This stone is said to bring you closer to those you love.

Beneficial for Concentration, cellular memory, diabetes, hypoglycaemia.

Datolite on matrix

Appearance	Chakra	Number	Zodiac sign
Transparent to opaque, vitreous crystal or mass	Heart, third eye, crown	5	Aries

Adamite

Properties If you are ruled or mortified by your emotions, Adamite will bring heart and mind together, providing objectivity, clarity and inner strength when dealing with emotional issues. If you have to focus on tasks or face difficult choices, this stone assists in consulting your inner self or in directing you to where the answers lie. The stone has a sense of humour and the answers might not be what you were expecting, but they work if you trust the process.

A creative stone, Adamite helps you to move forward confidently into an unknown future and brings to the fore entrepreneurial skills and the ability to identify new avenues for growth in both business and personal life. It is the perfect stone to programme to attract a new job or prosperity or simply to bring more joy into your life.

Beneficial for Cellular memory, endocrine system, glands, heart, lungs, throat.

Crystals on matrix

Appearance	Chakra	Number	Zodiac sign
Vitreous, transparent crystal or druse	Solar plexus, heart, throat	8	Cancer

Agrellite

Properties Agrellite surfaces things fast and may need other crystals or a qualified crystal healer. It shows where you have attempted to control others and supports you in allowing them independence and self-respect. Bringing to your attention matters that you have repressed and buried deep within your psyche, and which are blocking your soul growth, it also helps you to face your own inner saboteur and to access untapped potential.

This stone detects blockages within the physical body or aura, to which it has a distinctive energetic response, although other crystals may be required to heal the condition. Agrellite enhances all types of healing and makes a patient more receptive to radionic treatment.

Beneficial for 'Writer's block', diagnosis, immune system, bruises, infections, chemotherapy, over-alkalinity.

Raw

Appearance	Chakra	Number	Zodiac sign
Pearly, striated opaque stone	Third eye and higher crown	8, 44	Aquarius

Barite

Properties Reputedly used by Native Americans to journey from the physical to the spiritual worlds, Barite stimulates dreaming and dream recall. If anonymity and stealth are required for ritual or shamanic working, Barite confers this. This stone assists in communicating your intuitive vision and heightens ability to organize and express your thoughts.

A strongly motivating stone, Barite benefits people whose energies are scattered or exhausted. A powerful transformer, it may bring about a catharsis in which old emotional patterns, hatreds and fears are thrown off (this is best done under the supervision of a qualified crystal therapist); other crystals may be required to restore equilibrium.

Barite enhances autonomy. If you have been at the beck and call of others, or conformed to their ideals instead of your own, Barite sets you free. It is beneficial for platonic friendships, intimacy and insight into relationships.

Beneficial for Interpersonal communication, boundaries, confusion, loyalty, vitality, focus, over-sensitivity to cold or temperature changes, memory, overcoming shyness, chronic fatigue, detoxification, vision, addictions, sore throat, calming the stomach.

Natural

Appearance	Chakra	Number	Zodiac sign
Vitreous clear crystal or fibrous mass	Heart, throat	1	Aquarius

Clevelandite

Properties Clevelandite is an excellent stone to bring about a profound life change as it helps you to move forward into the future with equanimity and provides safe passage for your journey.

It helps you to focus on exactly what kind of change you need to bring about and shows you the gifts and tools you have at your disposal to assist in manifesting it. A stone of initiation for that journey, Clevelandite links to the three phases of the goddess and womanhood: maiden, mother and crone, facilitating transition and bringing about rebirth. It is the perfect stone for croning ceremonies.

Clevelandite also assists in turning difficult circumstances into positive, life-affirming situations. Placed on the solar plexus, it releases and transforms deeply held emotional fears of abandonment, rejection and betrayal or the consequences of such experiences, and facilitates nurturing yourself.

Beneficial for Puberty, menopause, cell membranes, cardiovascular disorders, joints, stroke.

Natural

Appearance	Chakra	Number	Zodiac sign
Opalescent, transparent to translucent blades	Sacral, base, third eye	4	Libra

Amblygonite

Properties A stone of balance, Amblygonite assists you to nurture yourself and to reconcile dualities, integrating the polarities of being. Strengthening self-worth, it awakens your sense of being a divine soul who is, therefore, immortal. A useful stone for gently releasing emotional hooks that have been embedded in the solar plexus in this or any other life. Amblygonite assists in ending relationships without angry consequences. It can be used to grid areas of discordance or public disorder, bringing peace and tranquillity, especially where young people are involved. In healing, Amblygonite activates the electrical systems of the body and can be taped over the thymus to protect against computer emanations in those who are sensitive.

This is a stone for the arts, promoting music, poetry and creativity of all kinds. It encourages empathy and thoughtfulness towards those around you.

Beneficial for Stress, genetic disorders, cellular memory, anxious stomach, digestion, headaches.

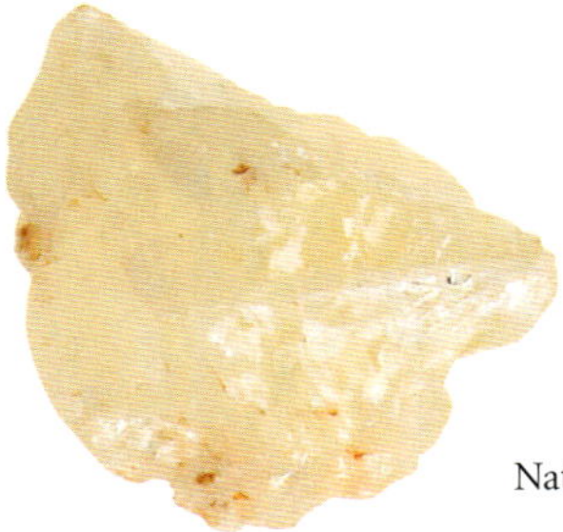

Natural

Appearance	Chakra	Number	Zodiac sign
Lustrous, opaque, very light colour	Solar plexus, higher crown, opens and aligns all	6	Taurus

Menalite

Properties Menalite reminds us of the endlessly recurring cycles of life and is excellent for rebirth and reincarnation and coming to terms with death. This deeply shamanic stone has been used for aeons of time to journey to other realms and carry out metaphysical work. Many of the stones simulate power animals or the ancient fertility goddess and this nurturing stone provides a durable link to the Earth Mother, taking you back into her womb. It also assists in remembering your soul.

Enhancing divination and forecasting, Menalite is an excellent stone for reconnecting to the wise feminine and to the power of the priestess. It is the perfect stone for conducting the rites of passage that mark out the transitions through womanhood. Keep one under your pillow during menopause and hold during a hot flush or night sweat.

Beneficial for Fertility, menopause, menstruation, lactation, night sweats.

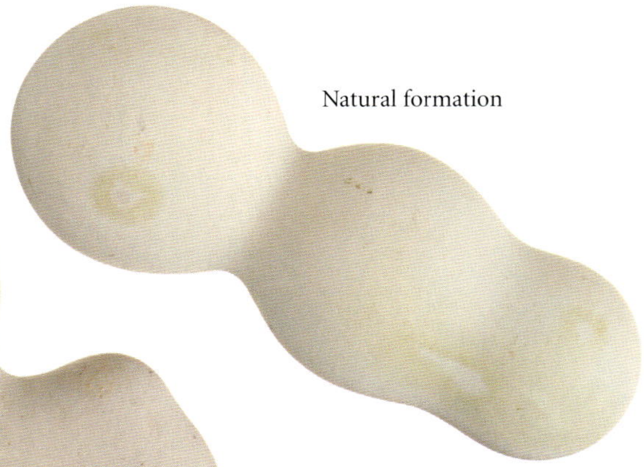

Natural formation

Natural formation

Appearance	Chakra	Number	Zodiac sign
Opaque, chalky white stone	Sacral	6	Cancer, Libra, Scorpio, Pisces

Pumice

Properties Although Pumice is not a crystal, it nevertheless is a powerful healer in certain situations. Placed over the thymus, it releases old pain held in the heart and gut, heals long-standing emotional wounds and reprogrammes emotional cellular memory. Pumice is particularly useful for defensive people who appear, on the surface, to be abrasive because of the pain they carry but who actually feel very vulnerable underneath the carapace. Promoting trust and acceptance, this stone gently assists in letting go protective barriers and accepting one's own vulnerability. It also increases the ability to let other people in and encourages intimacy on all levels.

Assisting toxin release during colonic hydrotherapy, Pumice can be used after the treatment to cleanse negative energy from the therapist and a large piece can be placed in any therapy room. Cleanse often.

Beneficial for Colonic hydrotherapy, detoxification, cellular memory, irritable bowel.

Shaped by sea

Appearance	Chakra	Number
Light, holey stone as though bubbles have burst (often found on beaches)	Higher heart (thymus)	4

Annabergite

Properties This crystal is elusive, appearing when the time is right. Annabergite brings with it the knowledge that everything is perfect exactly as it is, helping you to accept your life, showing you the harmony of your highest self and opening all possibilities, especially for healing. Placed on the third eye, this mystical stone is excellent for enhancing visualization and intuition, and for bringing contact with wise masters of the universe. Placed on the soma chakra, it enables you to know who you truly are and to reflect this to the world.

Aligning the aura and strengthening the biomagnetic energies, Annabergite enhances the flow of energy in the physical meridians and harmonizes these with the Earth's meridian grid, facilitating multidimensional cellular healing. It is said that Annabergite prepares the body to receive radiotherapy treatment and fight infections, and that it enhances receptivity when undergoing radionic treatment.

Beneficial for Cellular memory, dehydration, tumours, cellular disorders, infections.

Tumbled

Appearance	Chakra	Number	Zodiac sign
Apple green opaque stone	Third eye, soma	6	Capricorn

Wavellite

Properties Wavellite is an excellent stone for emotional healing and for clearing the effects of trauma or abuse from the emotional body, whether from the present or previous lives. It facilitates deep soul healing and provides an overview of situations and attitudes that lead to dis-ease, reprogramming cellular memory. This stone assists in maintaining health and wellbeing. Said to be at its most effective at the new moon, Wavellite can be used as a meditation tool at this time to access deep core issues and to intuitively know the way forward.

If you need an overview of a situation before making a move, hold Wavellite, which will also assist you to manage challenging situations with ease.

Beneficial for Energy flow from auric to physical bodies, cellular memory, blood flow, white cell count, dermatitis.

Natural formation

Natural

Appearance	Chakra	Number	Zodiac sign	Planet
Pearly, vitreous, roseate or radial crystalline needles	Past life, soma, heart, higher heart, solar plexus	1	Aquarius	Moon

Actinolite

Properties Uplifting Actinolite is an excellent stone for psychic shielding. Expanding the aura and crystallizing its edges, this stone connects you to higher awareness and brings body, mind, psyche and spirit into balance. An effective aid to visualization and imagery, it expands spontaneous creativity. Useful if you have encountered blockages or personal resistance on your spiritual path, Actinolite has been called the 'less is more' stone as it decreases and dissolves that which is unwanted or inappropriate, offers a new orientation and enhances self-esteem.

Bringing all physical functions into harmony and stimulating growth, Actinolite assists the body to adjust to changes or traumas.

Black Actinolite can be programmed to remove gently all that is outworn and outgrown, opening the way for new energies to manifest. It is an excellent stone for shielding yourself against your own negative thoughts.

Beneficial for Stress, asbestos-related cancers, the immune system, liver, kidneys.

Raw

Appearance	Chakra	Number	Zodiac sign
Translucent to transparent, vitreous, long-bladed crystals or compact opaque mass, may be included in Quartz	Heart, solar plexus, third eye, base (Black Actinolite)	4, 9	Scorpio, Capricorn (Black Actinolite)

Astrophyllite

Properties Astrophyllite is an excellent stone for promoting out-of-body experiences, acting as a guide and protector in other realms, but it also assists you in standing outside yourself for an objective view. This stone introduces you to your full potential, encouraging you to recognize that you have no limits. Astrophyllite activates your dreams and enables you to 'dream true' to see your soul path.

Emotionally, Astrophyllite eliminates without guilt anything that is outworn, showing you the way forward and assisting in completing projects. It reminds you that as one door closes, another opens.

Said to increase the sensitivity of touch and to improve the faculty of perception, Astrophyllite is helpful for those undergoing training in massage or acupressure, especially as it makes you more sensitive to other people's unspoken needs.

Beneficial for Inspiration, openness, large intestine, epilepsy, PMS and menopausal disturbances, reproductive and hormonal systems, cellular regeneration, fat deposits.

Tumbled stones

Appearance	Chakra	Number	Zodiac sign
Metallic or pearly blades	Higher crown	9	Scorpio

Eudialyte

Properties A personal-power stone imbued with life force, Eudialyte chases away depression and dissatisfaction with yourself, releasing the negative emotions that lie behind this. The ideal stone to promote self-forgiveness and healthy self-love, it expedites profound change and assists in learning from apparent mistakes. If you are angry at God, Eudialyte brings about reconciliation.

Connecting spirit and mind with the emotional body, it brings about reorientation of your inner being. This stone reunites soul-companions. If you have met a 'soulmate' who, seemingly, does not want to know; or someone to whom you are strongly attracted but question whether a sexual relationship is what you are destined for or whether there is spiritual work to do, meditating or sleeping with Eudialyte under the pillow will reveal the answer.

Beneficial for Energy depletion, forgiveness, jealousy, anger, guilt, resentment, animosity, confidence, brainwaves, multidimensional cellular healing, optic nerve.

Tumbled

Polished

Appearance	Chakra	Number	Zodiac sign
Mottled, opaque to transparent stone	Heart, links base and heart, opens and aligns all	3	Virgo

Epidote

Properties Not everyone responds to Epidote but for those who are attuned to it, Epidote enhances perception and personal power. It is said to increase spiritual attunement and to remove ingrained resistance to spiritual awakening and can support other spiritual stones in layouts.

Epidote purifies the emotional body and relieves negative states such as self-pity and anxiety. It releases grief, and assists you in staying centred no matter the situation you find yourself in. Its regenerative effect may create a powerful detoxification of negative energy from the aura, which can be experienced as a once-and-for-all catharsis or abreaction that clears the emotional blueprint and cellular memory. This use is best undertaken under the supervision of a crystal therapist.

Offering the courage to enjoy life to the full and the ability to manifest your dreams, Epidote strengthens your sense of identity. A useful stone in convalescence, it supports the body's healing processes and helps you to look after yourself in the best way possible.

Epidote is the perfect stone for those who easily fall into victimhood or martyrdom, dispelling criticism and self-criticism, and enabling you to look objectively at your own strengths and weaknesses and those of other people. Teaching you how to set realistic goals, it moves you away from unattainable expectations and inevitable failure and disappointments.

Beneficial for Emotional trauma, stamina, nervous and immune systems, cellular memory, dehydration, brain, thyroid, liver, gallbladder, adrenal glands. As an elixir it softens the skin.

Tumbled

Appearance	Chakra	Number	Zodiac sign
Vitreous mass or translucent crystals	Heart	2	Gemini

Shiva Lingam

Properties Symbolizing the god Shiva and union with his consort, Kali, a Shiva Lingam is traditionally used to raise and control kundalini energy and to facilitate spiritual evolution. This stone has been sacred for thousands of years as a symbol of sexuality and potent male energy. Excellent for sexual healing, it facilitates union of opposites such as masculine and feminine or body and soul. Suitably programmed, a Shiva Lingam severs etheric sexual connection after a relationship has ceased and removes hooks from vagina or uterus, re-energizing the base chakras and opening the way for a new relationship.

A stone of insight, Shiva Lingham facilitates looking within so that you release all that is outgrown. This stone is particularly useful for emotional pain that arises from early childhood, especially from sexual abuse, as meditated with daily it reinstates trust in male energy.

Beneficial for Effects of previous sexual mortification, infertility, impotence, inorgasmia, menstrual cramps.

Naturally shaped

Appearance	Chakra	Zodiac sign
Smooth, opaque two-coloured phallic shape	Base and sacral	Scorpio

Celestobarite

Properties Celestobarite is a shamanic oracle that shows you both sides of the coin, elucidating issues that are not clear, but leaving you to decide what to believe. This stone has a 'joker', coyote energy that presents the dark side in a joyful way and reminds us that nothing stays the same. Its Janus face looks to past, present and future and explores the multidimensional layers of being. With strong shielding energy, this is an excellent journeying stone that holds you suspended between the base and crown chakras and takes you safely into the shamanic middle world that lies parallel to the everyday world in which reside soul aspects and entities. Celestobarite cuts through edges and takes you to the edge and beyond.

Raw sliced

Appearance	Chakra	Number	Zodiac sign
Banded stone incorporating Barite and other crystals	Solar plexus, base and crown	8	Libra

Pyrophyllite

Properties Pyrophyllite, a form of kaolin, encourages autonomy and is useful for people who have psychological or psychic boundaries that are easily breached or that are too diffuse. If you do not recognize where you end and another person begins, or if you are easily swayed, hold a piece of Pyrophyllite in front of your solar plexus and it will help you to ascertain your boundaries and teach you to say 'no' when appropriate to those who try to control you. It is also helpful if you need to renegotiate promises or obligations that keep you attached to another person.

Because Pyrophyllite is delicate, it is unsuitable to wear in non-tumbled form, but can be kept by the bed or meditated with for 20 minutes a day to strengthen and crystallize the edges of your aura.

Beneficial for Indigestion, heartburn, over-acidity, diarrhoea.

Natural

Appearance	Chakra	Number	Zodiac sign
Fan-like crystals on a matrix	Sacral and solar plexus	8	Pisces

Goethite

Properties Goethite resonates to the master number 44, the number of metamorphosis and transmutation. This angel-attuned stone eliminates distractions, creating profound stillness that takes you to a point of non-action and non-doing. Conversely, it supplies the energy necessary for discovery and exploration of the human journey – and enjoyment of the process. Increasing divinatory powers, Goethite illuminates the future where this is helpful for your soul journey. An excellent communication tool, particularly if articulating your thoughts is difficult, this stone combines inspiration with pragmatic ability to get things done and facilitates clairaudience, enhances dowsing abilities and allows you to attune to the note of the Earth. It is said that gridding an area with Goethite will encourage a spaceship landing.

Iridescent Rainbow Goethite cuts through dark clouds, especially gloom and despondency, bringing light and hope into your life.

Beneficial for Weight training, epilepsy, anaemia, menorrhagia, ears, nose, throat, alimentary canal, veins, oesophagus.

Natural

Appearance	Chakra	Number	Zodiac sign
Transparent to translucent striated or needle-like crystals or stars	Clears base and aligns all	44 8	Aries

Bustamite

Properties A powerful energy worker, often found in conjunction with Sugilite (see page 162), Bustamite provides deep connection to the Earth and facilitates Earth healing, realigning the meridians of the Earth's etheric body. It is an excellent stone for gridding out a safe space in which to carry out ritual work, initiation or meditation. Realigning the energy meridians of the physical and subtle bodies, at the emotional level it removes old pain, harmonizing the emotional energy system and healing cellular memory. Stimulating conscious dreaming and intuition, Bustamite enhances channelling and accesses the angelic realms.

This stone creates inner congruency, assisting you to remove yourself mentally from disharmonious situations while remaining physically present, or to absent yourself physically from detrimental situations. It turns ideals and ideas into positive action. When Bustamite assists with your healing, you follow your life path with vigour. It is said to lose its lustre in the presence of danger.

Beneficial for Composure, cellular memory, stress-related illness, fluid retention, legs and feet, circulation, headaches, heart, skin, nails, hair, motor nerves and muscle strength, spleen, lungs, prostate gland, pancreas, calcium deficiencies.

Tumbled

Appearance	Chakra	Number	Zodiac sign
Vitreous, opaque and patterned	Base and sacral, heart and third eye, aligns all	2	Libra

Aegirine

Properties An excellent crystal for generating and focusing energy beams for use in healing a person or environment, Aegirine removes emotional energy blockages and enhances positive vibrations. Extremely helpful in psychic attack or negative thinking, it repairs the aura after attachments have been removed and turns negative thoughts positive, blocking mental influences. This stone helps you see the bigger picture and Aegirine heals relationship problems and overcomes the grief of separation. Encouraging sincerity in all that you do, Aegirine empowers the quest for your true Self and the ability to do what is needed from the heart.

This stone encourages following your own truth without conforming to the ideas or ideals of others, or to group pressure, and focuses your goals wisely. Boosting the body's self-healing systems, it enhances the healing energy of other crystals.

Beneficial for Integrity, self-esteem, cellular memory, the immune system, muscles and muscle pain, bones, metabolism, nerves.

Wand

Raw

Appearance	Chakra	Number	Zodiac sign
Transparent to opaque, long, green-red or black crystal, sometimes striated	Higher heart (thymus)	5	Pisces

Lepidocrocite

Properties Stimulating the mind and grounding your Self in everyday reality, Lepidocrocite aids recognizing your strengths at whatever level these occur. Heightening intuition, it acts as a bridge between matter and consciousness, encouraging practical application of spiritual insights. Cleansing the aura, it dissolves mental confusion, negativity, aloofness and disparity, replacing these with love whether for yourself, the environment or humanity.

Lepidocrocite enables you to observe without judgement and to teach without dogma, strengthening ability to empower others without entering into power issues yourself. It gives you the strength to stay the course and to make commitments to your life journey and the work you must do.

Beneficial for Enhancing healing energy of other stones, appetite suppression, liver, iris, reproductive organs, tumours, cellular regeneration.

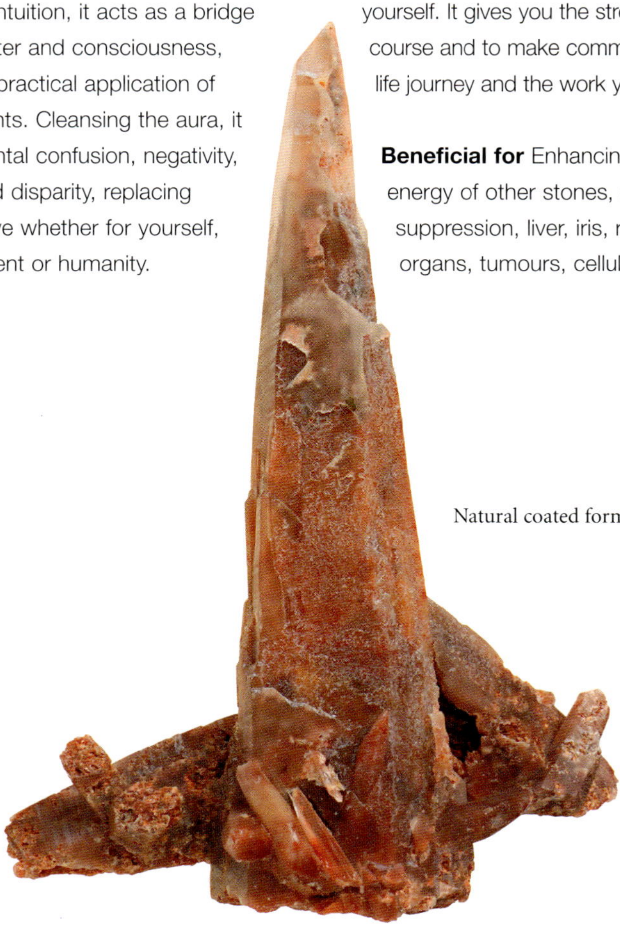

Natural coated formation

Appearance	Chakra	Number	Zodiac sign
Crusty opaque crystals or reddish inclusions	Aligns and stimulates all	8	Sagittarius

Cacoxenite

Properties One of the stones of ascension, Cacoxenite heightens spiritual awareness and assists planetary alignments to stimulate the vibratory evolution of Earth. Used in meditation or past-life regression, Cacoxenite takes you to the core soul memories into which insight is essential for present-day spiritual evolution to occur. Accentuating the positive in all that you do, it assists you to release restrictions and inhibitions, harmonizing the personal will with the higher self. If you have insurmountable problems confronting you, Cacoxenite creates a haven of peace to withdraw into, encouraging you to see events in a positive light.

Included within Amethyst, Cacoxenite activates the third eye and crown chakras, opening the mind to receive new ideas. This crystal heightens the power of full- or new-moon rituals and is a component of Super Seven (see pages 166–167).

Beneficial for Stress, holistic healing and psychosomatic awareness, cellular memory, fear, stress, hormonal and cellular disorders, heart, lungs, cold, flu, respiratory ailments.

Polished

Appearance	Chakra	Number	Zodiac sign
Radiated, feathery inclusion	Third eye, crown	9	Sagittarius

Creedite

Properties Creedite attunes you to a high spiritual vibration and assists in clarifying channelled messages and impressions received from the higher planes. Said to assist in linking to the universal wisdom embodied in ancient texts, it enhances communication and understanding of wisdom at any level. Creedite facilitates out-of-body experiences, guiding the soul to its destination and promoting total recall of the experience. Orange Creedite imparts urgency to spiritual evolution, speeding up the ability to move between the multidimensional levels of consciousness and attuning the physical body to the changing vibration.

Beneficial for Fractures, torn muscles and ligaments, stabilizing the pulse, assimilation of A, B and E vitamins.

Crystalline

Raw

Appearance	Chakra	Number	Zodiac sign
Transparent to opaque or needle-like crystals set on a matrix	Throat, crown	6	Virgo

Uranophane

Properties A radioactive crystal, Uranophane should be stored away from crystals that could be affected by its energetic vibration (it can be kept wrapped in aluminium foil or placed on Malachite). This is not a mineral to use for prolonged periods, nor for general healing. However, under the supervision of a suitably qualified practitioner, it supports nuclear-based medicine and radiation therapy, and acts as a homoeopathic catalyst for releasing past life and environmental radiation damage.

Uranophane subtly realigns the vibrations of the biomagnetic sheath so that energy shifts can be assimilated into the physical and etheric bodies.

Beneficial for Tumours, radiation damage.

Raw on matrix

Appearance	Chakra	Number	Zodiac sign
Hair-like crystals carried on a matrix	Past life, soma, cleanses all	5	Scorpio

Halite

Properties Halite is a stone of purification, symbolizing spiritual discernment and stimulating multidimensional evolution. Drawing out impurities and creating inner balance, it assists you in harnessing your will to the guidance of your spiritual Self and creates a more objective perspective.

Protecting against negative energies, entity attachment or psychic attack, Halite dissolves old behaviour patterns, negative thoughts and ingrained feelings such as anger, and can be placed in the bath for this purpose – however, be aware that the stone will dissolve and rock salt (a form of Halite) can be used in its place as it will be equally effective.

Ameliorating feelings of abandonment or rejection, this stone promotes well-being and increases goodwill. Affording effective protection at all times, Halite is said to prevent inadvertent spirit possession if you are under the influence of alcohol or drugs. This stone helps you transcend your problems and shows how to apply ancient-learned solutions to current situations, facilitating transmutation.

Because of its fragility, Halite cannot easily be worn but may be placed in your immediate environment or carefully wrapped in a pouch. As it quickly absorbs negative energy and damp, Halite should be cleansed frequently in brown rice and kept in a dry place.

Halite stimulates the meridians of the body and enhances acupuncture or acupressure, grounding the healing properties of other crystals.

Pink Halite is a useful tool for detaching entities and spirit possessions at all levels, and for preventing reattachment, or attachment of new spirits. Encouraging spiritual development, it stimulates metaphysical abilities and removes negativity. Pink Halite can be placed in the environment to facilitate well-being and a sense of being loved. It dispells oppression and acts as a diuretic.

Blue Halite opens the metaphysical gates, heightens intuition and encourages mystical awareness. This stone is extremely useful for reprogramming a distorted vision of reality and for cleansing mental attachments or undue influence from the third eye. It is helpful for acting on the thyroid, thymus, thalamus and with iodine absorption.

Appearance	Chakra	Number	Zodiac sign
Fragile, crusty, transparent small or large cubic crystals	Crown (Pink Halite) Third eye (Blue Halite), Heart (Pink Halite)	1	Cancer (pink) Pisces (blue)

Beneficial for Contentment, anxiety, detoxification, metabolism, cellular memory, water retention, intestinal problems, bi-polar disorders, respiratory disorders, skin.

Pink Halite

Vivianite

Properties Vivianite is the stone for crop-circle enthusiasts as it links into Earth energies and assists in reading crop markings and contacting the energy behind the patterns. If you want to integrate crop circle energy into your life, meditate with Vivianite in the centre of a crop circle or gaze into a photograph of a formation.

This stone is much more than appears at first glance and it has a 'quietly booming' energy. It is helpful for uncovering your deepest emotions and the things you deny to yourself. Vibrant Vivianite is a useful auric cleanser as, with its strong drawing power, it sucks out excess stimulation and negative energy, replacing it with peace and calm. It reverses the spin of the crown chakra if required, bringing in a base note and connecting to the subtle body of the Earth. This stone is the perfect adjunct to healing visualizations and to ritual working at a distance as it brings the souls together and enhances the effect.

An excellent healer for chronic eye conditions such as inflammation of the iris, Vivianite works with the third eye also to sharpen intuition and to act as a guide when travelling through the multidimensional planes of reality.

Vivianite's sparkling planes assist with dreamwork, drawing you back into the dream to find a deeper understanding and to rework the dream creatively to provide healing and insight.

Vivianite assists in setting and attaining realistic goals and imparts the strength to carry on through adversity, making life appear stimulating and challenging rather than dreary. If your relationship needs a shake-up, Vivianite is the stone to bring about revitalization.

Beneficial for Memory, increasing vitality, cellular memory, removing free radicals, assimilation of iron, spinal alignment, iritis, eyes, heart, liver.

Appearance	Chakra	Number	Zodiac sign
Small, transparent or metallic clusters or plates, crystals are sometimes bent	Earth, crown, third eye, soma	3	Capricorn

Natural formation on matrix

Leopardskin Serpentine

Properties Leopardskin Serpentine is a tactile stone that responds to holding rather than placement on the body. A shamanic stone, it assists you to access Leopard energy and to travel with the Leopard as a power or healing animal, or to shape-shift. As such, it is of enormous assistance in reclaiming power, especially where this has been misplaced or stolen in previous lives or in other dimensions.

With its powerful grounding energy, Leopardskin Serpentine keeps you earthed while opening shamanic consciousness and undertaking otherworld journeys and facilitates trancework and meditation, opening a direct channel to spiritual guidance. It offers insights into why you are living the life you are and assists with any adjustments that may be necessary to align with your soul plan for the present lifetime.

Tumbled

Appearance	Chakra
Leopard-like opaque stone	Third eye, soma, past life

Gaia Stone

Properties Manufactured from ash from Mount St Helen, USA, Gaia Stone is named for the ancient Greek Earth Mother goddess and is also known as the Goddess Stone. It shares properties with Obsidian, a volcanic glass without boundaries or limitations that allows energy to move rapidly through and which expels hidden matters to the surface for transformation, although Gaia Stone is gentler in its effects. Like Obsidian, it draws emotional wounds out of the body and can neutralize past trauma, replacing negativity with unconditional love.

Gaia Stone is said to link to the devas and the *anima terra*, the soul of the Earth. A stone of prosperity, Gaia Stone brings you into close harmony with the Earth and the environment and assists in healing the etheric energy grid of the planet, especially when gridded around areas of disharmony or pollution. This stone stimulates healing ability of all kinds and promotes compassion and empathy.

Beneficial for Self-healing, emotional wounds, past trauma.

Cut and polished stones

Appearance	Chakra	Number	Zodiac sign
Clear bright green crystal, like glass	Earth, heart, harmonizes all	9	Taurus

Cassiterite

Properties Traditionally linked to astrology and astronomy, Cassiterite imparts the mathematical precision and insights needed to see into the heart of a problem. An excellent stone for those suffering from rejection, abandonment, prejudice or alienation, or who were severely disapproved of in childhood or other situations, it gently dissolves resulting pain, especially where this underlies eating disorders or compulsive behaviour. Affording protection and encouraging healthy love of oneself, Cassiterite reminds you of your inherent perfection.

This stone assists you to perceive objectively how and why things were as they were, opening the way for compassion and forgiveness for all concerned and for cellular memory healing. It encourages you to do exactly what is necessary and no more for yourself and others, facilitating tough love if called for. With the assistance of Cassiterite, you can manifest your dreams and hopes for the future.

Beneficial for Eating disorders, obesity, malnutrition, cellular memory, nervous and hormonal systems, controlling secretions.

Raw on matrix

Appearance	Chakra	Number	Zodiac sign
Small prismatic or pyramidal crystals	Sacral, solar plexus, heart	2	Sagittarius

Cavansite

Properties Cavansite brings optimism and inspiration into your life, combining channelling and psychic awareness with pragmatic everyday learning and logical thought. Encouraging conscious astral journeying, this life-affirming crystal facilitates past-life exploration, reframing trauma at source so that it does not manifest in the present. A self-reflective stone, Cavansite redresses destructive behaviour or thought patterns, enabling you to be comfortable in your physicality.

Said to facilitate endorphin release, enhancing cellular healing, Cavansite shields a healer or past-life therapist during a session. Safeguarding your home or car, it sensitizes you to the need to look after the environment and instils an appreciation of the beauty all around. Cavansite helps you to think before you act.

Beneficial for Self-respect, purification, regeneration, cellular memory, recurrent disease, stabilizing the pulse, cellular healing, tinitus, eyes, teeth, sore throat, kidneys, bladder, fragmented 12-strand DNA, eyes, blood, calcium deficiency, teeth, joint flexibility.

Tumbled stones

Raw on matrix

Appearance	Chakra	Number	Zodiac sign
Translucent to transparent, vitreous, crystalline or pearly radial spheres, rosettes or fans on a matrix	Third eye, throat, past life	5	Aquarius

Dumortierite

Properties This substantial stone makes you more receptive when communicating with angelic or spirit guides and assisting you to see the worth in each human being. Placed immediately behind the ear, it opens clairaudience. An excellent stone for past-life work, Dumortierite takes you to the beginning of your soul journey to examine the soul contracts and agreements made over aeons of time, renegotiating or releasing these if no longer applicable. Placed on the soma or past-life chakras, it stimulates regression and recall, assists the breaking of old ties that no longer serve, and facilitates rescinding vows. Showing you your archetypal spiritual Self, it reconnects to your innate wisdom. Dumortierite is particularly useful for identifying and releasing past-life causes of dis-ease, difficult circumstances or relationships in the present life, and the patterns that underlie addictions and compulsions so that cellular memory can be reprogrammed.

Instilling an instinct for self-preservation and unshakeable self-confidence, Dumortierite assists in standing up for yourself and adapting to present reality, offering patience or courage if required. It also calms over-excitability, promotes detachment, and instils a positive self-love and *joie de vivre*. Enhancing organizational abilities and focus, Dumortierite helps you to remain young at heart and is excellent for developing a positive attitude to life.

This stone helps to stabilize a rocky relationship and is said to attract a soulmate – although there may be difficult lessons to learn in the process. A useful stone for people who deal with crisis and trauma on a daily basis, it creates a calming effect and focuses relief efforts. If you are chaotic and disorganized, Dumortierite helps to take control of your life. It is the stone *par excellence* for efficient filing. This stone is said to assist in developing your linguistic capabilities so that you can communicate with other cultures.

Beneficial for Stage fright, shyness, stress, phobias, insomnia, panic, fear, depression, patience, self-discipline, mental clarity, stubbornness, cellular memory, sunburn, hypersensitivity, wasting disorders, epilepsy, headaches, nausea, vomiting, cramp, colic, diarrhoea, palpitations.

Appearance	Chakra	Number	Zodiac sign
Dense, dusty, mottled opaque stone with iridescent flashes, blue inclusion, or crystalline	Past life, throat, third eye, soma	4	Leo

Polished stones

Raw

Covellite

Properties A stone of intent connecting to the higher self, Covellite is helpful in transforming dreams into realities and opening your metaphysical abilities. Covellite is reflective and opens a doorway to the past and to the wisdom you acquired at that time bringing it forward into the present. It also helps you to release anything holding you in the past, particularly ingrained beliefs or cellular programmes. Covellite facilitates the flow of energy through cells. It harmonizes body, mind and soul and helps you to love yourself unconditionally while eliminating vanity.

Covellite is said to protect the body against radiation and to banish arrogance. Useful if you feel vulnerable and too easily stimulated by others, or suffer from discontent, Covellite instils well-being and satisfaction with life. This stone facilitates rational analytic thought and the decision-making process.

Beneficial for Communication, creativity, rebirthing, cellular memory, sexuality, detoxification, despondency, anxiety, birth, rebirth, digestion, cancer, ears, eyes, nose, mouth, sinuses, throat.

Tumbled

Appearance	Chakra	Number	Zodiac sign
Lustrous, metallic opaque stone, sometimes tarnished	Third eye, sacral, solar plexus	4, 7	Sagittarius

Blue Aragonite

Properties Carrying the generic Earth-healing and grounding properties of Aragonite, beautiful Blue Aragonite is coloured by copper, the Venus metal that is a powerful energy conduit, and it both heightens and grounds spiritual communication. This loving stone purifies and aligns all the subtle bodes with the physical, and balances yin-yang energies, leading to optimum well-being and making you comfortable within your physical body. It is a powerful Earth- and soul-healer and can be gridded around houses to keep the environment stable and harmonious. Blue Aragonite is excellent for inner-child work and for manifesting your soul plan for the present life. If you wish to attract your spiritual twinflame, programme Blue Aragonite to manifest this for you.

This stone instils a sense of resolute optimism and patience, uplifts your emotions and assists you to find insights into the source of any problems you may be encountering, turning them into opportunities to grow.

Beneficial for Geopathic stress, cellular memory, Reynauds disease, spasm.

Raw

Raw

Appearance	Chakra	Zodiac sign
Blue, opaque stone (may be dyed)	Third eye, throat, heart	Capricorn

Tanzanite

Properties With a high vibration that facilitates altered states of consciousness, inner and outer journeying, metaphysical abilities and profoundly deep meditation, Tanzanite links to the angelic realms, spirit guides, Ascended Masters and Christ consciousness. Facilitating living consciously in the now, Tanzanite opens subtle chakras on the aura to access the next level of spiritual evolution. Downloading information from the Akashic Record, when combined with Iolite and Danburite, Tanzanite brings about multidimensional cellular healing. Ascertaining your true vocation, it is beneficial for overworked people, smoothing fluctuations of energy and assisting in taking time for yourself. Tanzanite jewellery should be worn with care as it may over-stimulate sensitive people. If it induces uncontrolled psychic experiences or mental overload from unwanted telepathy, remove and replace with an appropriate protection stone.

Beneficial for Reprogramming cellular memory, past-life healing, hearing, trust, cellular memory, workaholics, depression, anxiety, poise, hair, skin, head, throat, chest, kidneys, nerves.

Raw

Artificially double terminated

Tumbled

Appearance	Chakra	Number	Zodiac sign
Bright faceted gem or slightly opaque	All, especially crown and higher crown to base, throat	2	Gemini, Libra, Sagittarius, Pisces

Scapolite

Properties Gazing into the depths of Blue Scapolite is extremely calming and assists in going deep within the Self to find the source of problems from this or another life. This stone rejigs the emotional blueprint, clearing the effects of old emotional trauma, and eliminating it from the emotional body, which then has a physical healing effect. Scapolite facilitates release of 'stuck energy' from the physical body, especially in the legs and veins, and removes blockages from the left-hand side of the brain, increasing analytic ability. Stimulating your ability to be independent and to set achievable goals, Blue Scapolite overcomes self-sabotage, induces transformation and provides the clarity to see what is needed in any situation. It is an excellent stone to programme if you wish to make conscious changes.

Beneficial for Dyslexia, post-operative recovery, cellular memory, calcium assimilation, varicose veins, restless legs, cataracts, glaucoma, bone disorders, shoulders, dyslexia, incontinence.

Cut and polished stones

Appearance	Chakra	Number	Zodiac sign
Transparent or translucent crystalline masses or columns	Throat, soma	1	Taurus

Youngite

Properties A transformative combination of stimulating yet calming Brecciated Jasper (a crystal composed of angular fragments), energetic Quartz and Drusy Quartz (see page 24), Youngite is a shamanic stone that accesses different planes of consciousness, taking you to a space without thought where souls meet and merge. From here it links to other planes of existence, touching supraconsciousness and all that it offers.

Excellent for inner-child work, Youngite reconnects to the joyous, innocent child that lies within everyone and the creative power that child offers. Healing wounds from childhood, Youngite is useful in soul retrieval and reintegration work as it gently coaxes back childish soul fragments that split off through joy or trauma. At the same time, Youngite is said to be an excellent stone for warriors and leaders as it lights the way.

The Brecciated Jasper component heals mental stress, centres the mind, and increases mental agility and rational thought, strengthening intellectual capability in difficult circumstances while the Drusy Quartz enhances the ability to laugh at the most traumatic of events.

Natural

Appearance	Chakra	Number	Zodiac sign
Tiny drusy crystals over a Jasper matrix	Solar plexus, heart	44	Gemini

Avalonite (Drusy Blue Chalcedony)

Properties Instilling peace and neutralizing negative thought patterns, Avalonite accesses the collective unconscious and mythical realms where fairy tales and legend offer deep wisdom, creatively reworking the myths in your life. Contacting fairies, elves and devas, it links into ancient magic. Use Avalonite to harmonize the emotional, mental and spiritual wisdom at the centre of your being. Following the contours of this beautiful stone enhances visualization, opens psychic awareness, and stimulates telepathy between soul partners. The depths of Avalonite gently transport you into your past to contact your wise woman or priestess incarnations. Enhancing practical wisdom and presence of mind, especially when faced with new situations, this stone is perfect for those who fear to love or who fear failure, opening the heart and allowing you to discover the perfection of your true Self, it recognizes that you are never alone. Avalonite absorbs negative energy and transmutes it to prevent onward transmission but requires regular cleansing and recharging.

Beneficial for Sensitivity to weather or pressure changes.

Geode

Appearance	Chakra	Number	Zodiac sign
Tiny crystals, almost velvety, often within a geode	Links sacral and heart	9	Pisces

Lazulite

Properties Lazulite is often called the Stone of Heaven. As with all blue stones, Lazulite draws in pure universal energy and opens intuition, bringing about profound states of meditative bliss. Lazulite creates a calm and serene Self, anchored in the divine.

Traditionally known as the worry stone, Lazulite gives insight into the cause of problems, and also provides intuitive solutions to the underlying cause. This stone assists in finding reasons behind addiction, particularly if these lie in previous lives, and in detaching from the desire for more. Boosting confidence and self-esteem, it promotes personal balance and alignment to the cosmos.

Beneficial for Sun-sensitivity, immune system, cellular memory, fractures, thyroid, pituitary, lymphatic system, liver.

Raw

Appearance	Chakra	Number	Zodiac sign
Grainy, dense mass with tiny pyramidal crystals	Throat, third eye	7	Gemini, Sagittarius

Purpurite

Properties Excellent for public speaking, Purpurite gives you clarity and confidence, safe in the knowledge that no outside influence can interfere with the dissemination of your views. Purpurite stimulates spiritual evolution and enlightenment and increases alertness and receptivity to guidance and new ideas.

Purpurite breaks old habits or attitudes that keep you imprisoned. Opening the higher crown chakras, it stimulates unimpeded evolution. This stone energizes the physical and mental bodies, overcoming tiredness and despondency at any level.

This stone has facilitated house sales where adverse environmental and community interference were blocking the sale and past-life conflict had been recreated. Dispersing negative energy from the environs, a curse was lifted and positive energy imprinted. Equally helpful in any sale situation, it can be programmed to find a buyer quickly.

Beneficial for Exhaustion, stamina, cellular memory, rejuvenation, despair, bruises, bleeding, pustules, cardio-thoracic system and blood flow, blood purification, stabilizing the pulse.

Cut and lightly polished

Appearance	Chakra	Number	Zodiac sign
Vivid banded and veined metallic opaque stone	Base, crown, higher crown	9	Virgo

Stichtite

Properties Stichtite supports you in manifesting your true Self and living in accord with your soul-contract for the present life. A beneficent stone to keep in your pocket if you live alone, it provides companionship and has a calming influence on the environment.

Traditionally, this stone aids the movement of the kundalini energy up the spine to the heart. Assisting in keeping your mind and opinions open, and your emotional awareness acute, it teaches you how your emotions and ingrained attitudes affect your well-being. If a child, or for that matter yourself, needs gently guiding on to a different path, Stichtite is the perfect tool, and it is excellent for indigo children who suffer from hyperactivity or similar spiritual dis-eases.

Beneficial for ADHD, skin elasticity and stretch marks, hernia, teeth and gums.

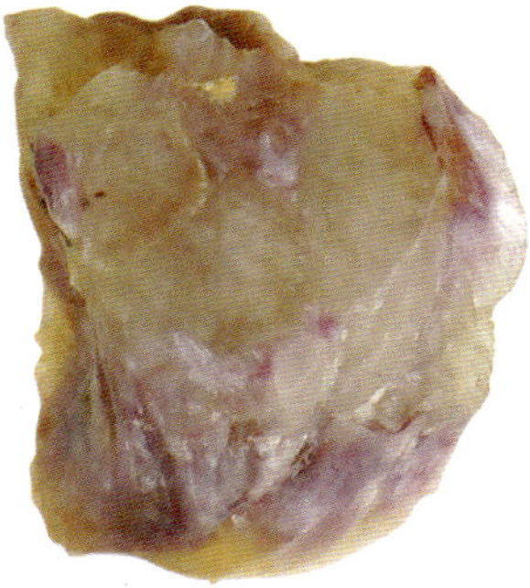

Natural form

Appearance	Chakra	Number	Zodiac sign
Waxy, opaque layers	Earth, base, heart, raises kundalini through all	5	Virgo

Atlantasite

Properties A combination of green Serpentine, an earthing stone that corrects emotional imbalances, assisting you to feel more in control of life, and which opens up psychic abilities, and purple Stichtite, Atlantasite is said to access past lives in Atlantis and to support in completing projects set in motion at that time.

Atlantasite aids those who misused their spiritual powers at that or any other time, teaches right use of will and stimulates spiritual evolution.

Atlantasite lowers stress levels and encourages you to think before you speak. It brings enormous peace into the environment and, buried in the earth, undertakes earth clearing and energy restructuring in a place where there has been death and destruction. This stone is helpful for gently encouraging children to modify inappropriate behaviour.

Beneficial for Cellular memory, stress, blood disorders, hypoglycaemia, diabetes.

Tumbled stones

Appearance	Chakra
Opaque combination of two clearly defined colours	Clears all, especially higher crown, crown, soma and heart

Hemimorphite

Properties Hemimorphite encourages the raising of the body's vibrations and communication with the highest spiritual levels and multi-dimensions. This crystal facilitates self-development in the quickest way possible so it is unlikely to create a smooth passage through life. A stone of personal responsibility, it links you to your higher self, encouraging acceptance and responsibility for your own happiness or dis-ease, and teaches that you create your own reality through thoughts and attitudes. It also helps you to recognize where you fall under outside influences that do not accord with your own soul-view, and to release from these.

This stone shows you how to develop your own inner strength and to manifest your highest potential, at the same time instilling a sense of social responsibility and awareness of being part of humanity. It is an excellent stone for remaining energized and committed throughout projects, seeing them through to the end.

Hemimorphite gently soothes emotional angst and supports in regaining full health on all levels. If you invariably pitch your expectations and goals too high to achieve success, Hemimorphite helps you to set and attain realistic goals.

This stone assists you to look back on, accept and reframe irritating traits, and facilitates your being totally open and honest in your emotional communication with yourself and others.

A Hemimorphite cluster is a beautiful object in its own right and can be used as a protective stone, particularly against malicious thoughts. In ancient times, it was reputedly used to counteract poisons of all kinds. Tumbled Hemimorphite is available for personal wear or healing placements.

Beneficial for Energy, optimism, weight loss, pain relief, blood disorders, heart, cellular memory, cellular structures, ulcerative conditions, burns, genital herpes, warts, restless legs.

Appearance	Chakra	Number	Zodiac sign
Tiny transparent needle-like striated or pyramidal crystals on a matrix, or botryoidal crust	Higher heart, higher crown, solar plexus, past life	4	Libra

Natural formation

Botryoidal crust

Crystalline form

Dalmatian Stone

Properties Dalmatian Stone helps you to get out of your head and into your body. This stone imparts a sense of physicality to the soul, reminding you that you are a spiritual being on a human journey. A grounding and centring aid, it assists in coming to terms joyfully with being incarnate and harmonizes your emotions. A protective influence, Dalmatian Stone is said to sound a warning when danger is near, and to assist in maintaining composure.

This playful stone helps you to avoid over-analysis, and moves you forward in life, but at the same time allows you to reflect on possible actions and to plan with care. A fortifying stone, it stimulates your sense of fun and is an excellent pick-me-up. As it contains Tourmaline, Dalmatian Stone transmutes negative energy and outworn patterns and can be kept in your pocket for long periods.

Beneficial for Animals, athletes, balancing yin-yang, mood elevation, nightmares, fidelity, cartilage, nerves and reflexes, sprains.

Tumbled

Appearance	Chakra	Number	Zodiac sign
Spotted opaque stone	Base, sacral, earth	9	Gemini

Chrysotile (Chrysotite, Chrysolite)

Properties Banded Chrysotile is an exceedingly visual stone. It is said to be one of the stones used in the 'breastplate' of the ancient Jewish High Priests. If you angle it, it is possible to see ancient writing inscribed upon it that links you to the knowledge of the ages and, below that, your power animal waiting to make itself known so that you can embody it. This deeply shamanic stone assists you to clear away the debris of the past to reveal your core Self. It also shows you where you seek to control others, assisting you to let that go while steering your own destiny.

In healing, placed over the thymus Chrysotile works on the etheric blueprint to correct imbalances and blockages that could manifest as physical disease and to heal cellular memory.

Beneficial for Chronic fatigue, irritating coughs, parathyroid, throat, brainstem, central meridian channel, emphysema, inflammation, multiple sclerosis.

Tumbled

Appearance	Chakra	Number	Zodiac sign
Concentric dark- and light-banded stone	Third eye	8, 55	Taurus

Ammolite

Properties A powerful Earth-healing stone, Ammolite was created by compression and mineralization of ammonite fossil, the brilliant colours being produced by Aragonite and trace minerals. Harmonious Ammolite contains the wisdom of the ancients and was worn on the forehead for consciousness activation, metaphysical powers and interdimensional exploration. It is particularly effective when placed on the soma chakra.

Representing coming full circle, Ammolite takes you into your centre and into completion. Activating your own personal empowerment, it converts negative energy into a gently flowing positive spiral. Ammolite stimulates survival instincts, helping you to know that you will get there if you persevere, and mapping your way with the lifepath encoded within.

Assisting anything that needs structure and clarity, Ammolite relieves birth trauma affecting the craniosacral flow and is helpful in all craniosacral work. A powerful karmic cleanser, it releases mental obsessions.

Feng Shui masters call Ammolite the Seven-Colour Prosperity Stone as it displays intense crimson, fiery orange, golden amber, vivid green, soothing jade, intense azure and brilliant mauve colours. They believe Ammolite absorbed cosmic energy over aeons of time and therefore stimulates the flow of *Qi*, life force, through the body. According to them, this stone is fortunate for anyone who comes in contact with it. Keep one in your home to bring wealth, health, vitality and a happy life; and in business premises to promote beneficial business dealings. As jewellery, the stone imparts charisma and sensuous beauty to the wearer.

In Feng Shui red represents growth and energy; orange represents creativity and increased libido; green represents wisdom, intellect, entrepreneurship; yellow represents wealth; and blue represents peace and health.

Beneficial for Longevity, awakening kundalini energy, cellular memory, prosperity, creativity, well-being, stamina, vitality, health, stabilizing the pulse, degenerative disorders, depression, labour pain, rebirthing, osteomyelitis, ostitis, tinnitus, cranium and inner ear, cell metabolism, lungs, limbs.

Appearance	Chakra	Number	Zodiac sign
Opalized ammonite shell or small, intensely coloured section	Third eye, soma	9	Aquarius

Polished

Slice

Alexandrite

Properties A guardian stone and useful purifier and renewer, Alexandrite confers longevity and protection, and harmonizes male and female energies. It inspires the imagination and attunes you to your own inner voice. An emotional comforter that facilitates emotional maturity, Alexandrite teaches how to expend less effort and find more joy in life. This regenerative stone rebuilds self-respect and self-worth, enhancing rebirth of one's Self, which it centres, reinforces and realigns. It intensifies your willpower and your dreams, and assists in accurately perceiving emotions – both your own and those of others. Alexandrite is traditionally used for jewellery, which needs cleansing regularly.

Worn over the heart, Alexandrite traditionally brings luck in love and is said to impart grace and elegance to the wearer.

Beneficial for Regeneration, nervous and glandular systems, inflammation, spleen, pancreas, liver, male reproductive organs, neurological tissue, tension in neck muscles, side-effects of leukaemia.

Faceted stones

Crystal on matrix

Raw

Appearance	Chakra	Zodiac sign	Planet
Shines red or green according to light source	Lower, heart	Scorpio	Pluto

Zircon

Properties In ancient times Zircon was used to protect against robbery, lightning, bodily harm and disease. Promoting unconditional love, this stone harmonizes your spiritual nature with the environment and brings all the systems of the physical and subtle bodies into alignment. It assists in recognizing the human journey of the soul and the oneness from which all souls originated. A stone of union, it brings together opposites and instils stamina and tenacity of purpose. Zircon overcomes jealousy and possessiveness and promotes letting go of old love.

This stone enhances clear thinking and helps to separate the significant from the insignificant. Overcoming prejudice and racism, Zircon teaches brotherhood of humanity and clears the effects of discrimination, victimization, homophobia and misogyny from the emotional body. Cubic Zircon (man-made) has considerably diluted powers.

Yellow Zircon assists you in attracting success in business and in love and enhances your sexual energy. It lifts depression and makes you more alert.

Green Zircon is an attractor of abundance.

Brown Zircon is excellent for centring and grounding.

Red Zircon lends vitality to the body, particularly during periods of stress. It is reputed to add power to rituals for creating wealth.

Orange Zircon makes an excellent talisman for use during travelling as it protects against injury. This stone is reputed to increase beauty and to guard against jealousy.

Beneficial for Synergy, constancy, sciatica, cramp, insomnia, depression, bones, muscles, vertigo, liver, menstrual irregularity. (Zircon may cause dizziness in those who wear pacemakers or those who are epileptic.)

Raw stones

Appearance	Chakra	Number	Zodiac sign	Planet
Faceted gemstone or translucent, often double-pyramid	Varies according to colour, unites base, solar plexus and heart	4	Sagittarius	Sun

Diopside

Properties An analytical stone that stimulates intellectual faculties, Diopside is helpful for academic study or for creative pursuits. Teaching humility and assisting in honouring what you really feel, it supports following your own intuition. Diopside increases compassion and humility, opening your heart to the suffering of others, and encourages you to be of service to the planet. Emotionally, Diopside is beneficial for those who cannot show their grief because it promotes letting go and forgiveness, and for those who feel overburdened because it teaches you how to live life with appreciation and *joie de vivre*.

This stone assists you in reconciling with anyone or anything that has hurt you in the past, facilitating your making the first approach if necessary.

Beneficial for Mathematics, trust, psychological conditions, cellular memory, physical weakness, acid-alkaline balance, inflammation, muscular aches and spasm, kidneys, heart, hormonal balance, circulation, blood pressure, stress.

Natural formation

Appearance	Chakra	Number	Zodiac sign
Transparent to opaque, deep-coloured crystal	Third eye, soma, heart	9	Virgo

Marcasite

Properties Marcasite expands your metaphysical abilities, especially that of spirit awareness and clairvoyance, while providing a psychic shield and grounding you in the everyday world. It especially assists and protects those who undertake house-clearing or entity removal but should be cleansed immediately. This stone increases objectivity, encouraging you to move to a more detached perspective when seeking insight into yourself or others, and helps you to make confidently any adjustments necessary for your growth.

If you suffer from scattered or confused thinking and impaired memory, Marcasite assists by bringing clarity to your mind. Increasing your willpower, it helps you to go boldly where you have not been before. This is an excellent stone for Leos because it encourages you to shine and it helps anyone who suffers from a sense of spiritual lack to find true abundance.

Beneficial for Yang energy, concentration, memory, hysteria, cleansing the blood, warts, moles, freckles, spleen.

Crystals on matrix

Appearance	Chakra	Number	Zodiac sign
Metallic masses or small crystals on a matrix	Base	8	Leo

Eilat Stone

Properties Combining Malachite, a transformative and protective stone that absorbs negative energy and highlights psychosomatic dis-ease; Turquoise, a purification stone and efficient healer and protector that brings solace to the spirit and opens psychic gifts; Chrysocolla, a tranquil and sustaining stone that assists with accepting change; Azurite, a stone of spiritual vision and new perspective; and other minerals, Eilat Stone instils a sense of wonder at the beauty all around. An excellent all-round healer, cleanser and conductor of energy, it is particularly effective for cleansing the thymus. Flushing out hurt and loss, it removes detritus and toxins created from soul-shattering events in current or previous lives. Bringing about acceptance and inner reconciliation, it calls the fragments home and wipes the Akashic Record clean, reprogramming soul and cellular memory.

Known as the 'sage stone' because it offers wisdom and creative solutions for problem-solving, Eilat Stone balances yin and yang and brings about a lightness of being. It harmonizes and yet stimulates your emotional life, ensuring that it is never dull and stimulates your creativity, encourages telepathy between soul partners, for which two stones are required.

Beneficial for Psychosomatic dis-ease, effects of incest, rape, physical violence, misogyny or sexual repression; radiation-related illness, fear, reintegration, fever, pain, depression, cellular memory, bone and tissue regeneration, strengthening meridians, sinus, reorders cellular growth rate, tumours, liver, menstrual cramps.

Appearance	Chakra	Number	Zodiac sign
Mottled, opaque stone	Higher heart, heart and throat; clears and balances all	3	Sagittarius

Polished

Raw

Bustamite with Sugilite

Properties Excellent for relieving migraine and headaches, especially where these stem from unused psychic ability, Bustamite with Sugilite increases spiritual and psychic awareness while remaining grounded, joining heaven and earth. The combined stone opens your intuition and improves your ability to listen to the voice of your Self.

The Sugilite component helps sensitive people adapt to being in the earth environment while keeping their spiritual connection open to nourish the core of their being, but this is an excellent stone for anyone who feels they do not fit in or is isolated in any way. It can be programmed to draw like-minded souls together and to channel more love into the earth.

Beneficial for Migraine, dyslexia, cellular memory, epilepsy, schizophrenia, paranoia.

Tumbled

Appearance	Chakra
Opaque mottled stone	Third eye, soma

Ajoite with Shattuckite

Properties An excellent energy conduit, this combination of Ajoite with Shattuckite is one of the most powerful protections against electromagnetic smog and psychic attack. Creating a protective bubble around the aura that keeps you safe no matter where you may be, it enables you to remain open spiritually.

In times of stress, wearing this stone allows you to experience profound peace and to remain centred in yourself (see also Ajoite, page 71).

Karmically, Ajoite with Shattuckite assists the process of atonement, reconciliation and reparation, releasing the need for such acts where these have become a blockage to spiritual progress, especially if a subtle carryover of past-life mortification practices. It teaches the difference between atonement and at-onement and opens the way for the karma of grace to operate.

Beneficial for Cellular memory, stress-related illness, bowel blockages, constipation.

Raw

Appearance	Chakra
Mottled Turquoise with Quartz and dark patches	Higher heart, third eye

Red Feldspar with Phenacite

Properties A deeply spiritual stone, Feldspar with Phenacite raises self-awareness and the ability to love yourself unconditionally. An extremely high vibration stone linked to the Akashic Record and spiritual masters, Phenacite is a purification tool for the etheric body and an aid to interdimensional travel. This combination stone is the key to changing your reality as it grounds spiritual insight into physical expression. The spirit of this stone is joyful, reminding you that spiritual evolution and life on Earth do not have to be taken too seriously and growth can be fun. The spirit of the stone accompanies you back into a dream pointing out the deeper implications as you go, reworking the dream to bring about a fruitful outcome.

The Feldspar constituent of this stone is extremely helpful in letting go of the past and especially of ingrained mental and spiritual patterns from past lives, reprogramming cellular memory and enabling the Phenacite to open the way to a much more dynamic way of being.

Beneficial for Unconditional love, overcoming mortification, repatterning the etheric blueprint, cellular memory, skin, muscular problems.

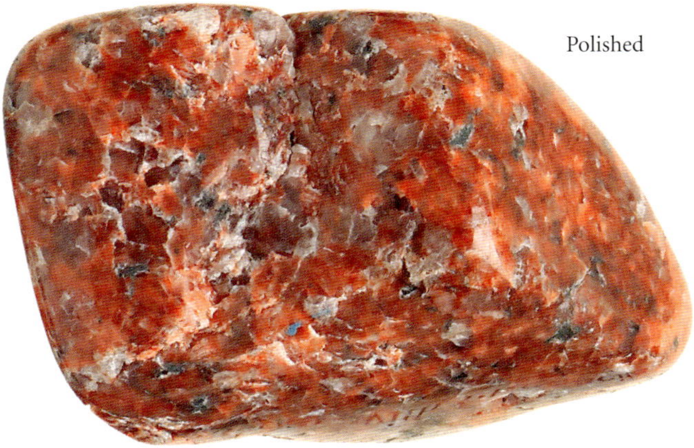

Polished

Appearance	Chakra
Opaque stone with clear inclusions and crystals	Third eye, higher heart, higher crown

Rutile with Hematite

Properties Rutile with Hematite brings together insight into psychosomatic causes of dis-ease with the cleansing properties of Rutile (see page 97) and the grounding and energizing functions of Hematite. This powerfully protective and regenerative stone assists with reconciliation and the bringing together of opposites. Whatever needs balancing in your life can be helped by this stone and it particularly assists with deep karmic and soul cleansing, repair of cellular memory, and interpersonal relationships.

Placed on the soma chakra, Rutile with Hematite attunes you to the true Self that is beyond duality or division and is helpful in calling dismembered parts of your soul home for integration into the whole. This stone can bring about profound multidimensional healing, cleansing and opening chakras up to the highest levels and bringing about a profound connection with the most refined vibrations in the universe. It is extremely effective placed on the soma chakra to harmonize spiritual and personal identity.

Natural formations

Appearance	Chakra	Zodiac sign
Beautiful silver and gold opaque stone	Past life, soma	Libra

Super Seven (The Melody Stone)

Properties A combination of protective Amethyst, Smoky Quartz, purifying Quartz, Rutile (see page 97), Goethite (see page 123), Lepidocrocite (see page 126) and Cacoxenite (see page 127) and reported by its finder, Melody, after whom it is sometimes named, to have the highest vibration of any crystal yet found, radiant Super Seven is a spiritual powerhouse with exceptional clarity. Shifting the vibratory level of the planet and everything upon it, this stone ushers in the Aquarian Age and can be programmed to bring about a radiant future.

Many pieces of Super Seven carry a spiritual being within them that links to the highest sources of guidance and inspiration. Meditating with it is a joy and it is a useful stone for programming to carry flower essences for distant healing.

An extremely soothing and nurturing crystal, Super Seven opens all the spiritual gifts and enhances metaphysical working of all kinds. Never requiring cleansing or re-energizing, it supports and heightens the vibration of any other crystal in its vicinity. This stone purifies, balances and energizes all the chakras and the auric bodies, aligning them to the most refined spiritual vibrations.

Super Seven is a powerful stone for healing physical, intellectual and spiritual dis-ease and for bringing the soul back into communication with the divine. The smallest piece of Super Seven carries the vibration of the whole whether or not all the minerals are present, reminding us that we too are part of a whole that is much more than the brotherhood of humanity.

Small points are now available that are extremely powerful for self-healing and for opening to spiritual realities. These points can also be used to pull stagnant energy out of the body, or to grid areas of disturbed earth or community energy, and are particularly useful where there is fear of terrorist activity or racial unrest, as they instil peace and a sense of communal safety and interconnection.

Beneficial for Harmonizing the body, cellular memory, immune system, healing the planetary grid, stimulating the body's natural healing system, skin, bones.

Appearance	Chakra	Zodiac sign
Clear to opaque swirling crystal with several colours visible	Harmonizes all	Unites all

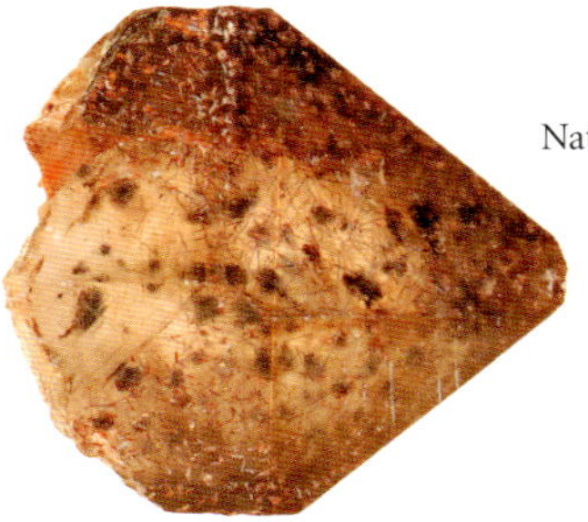

Natural point

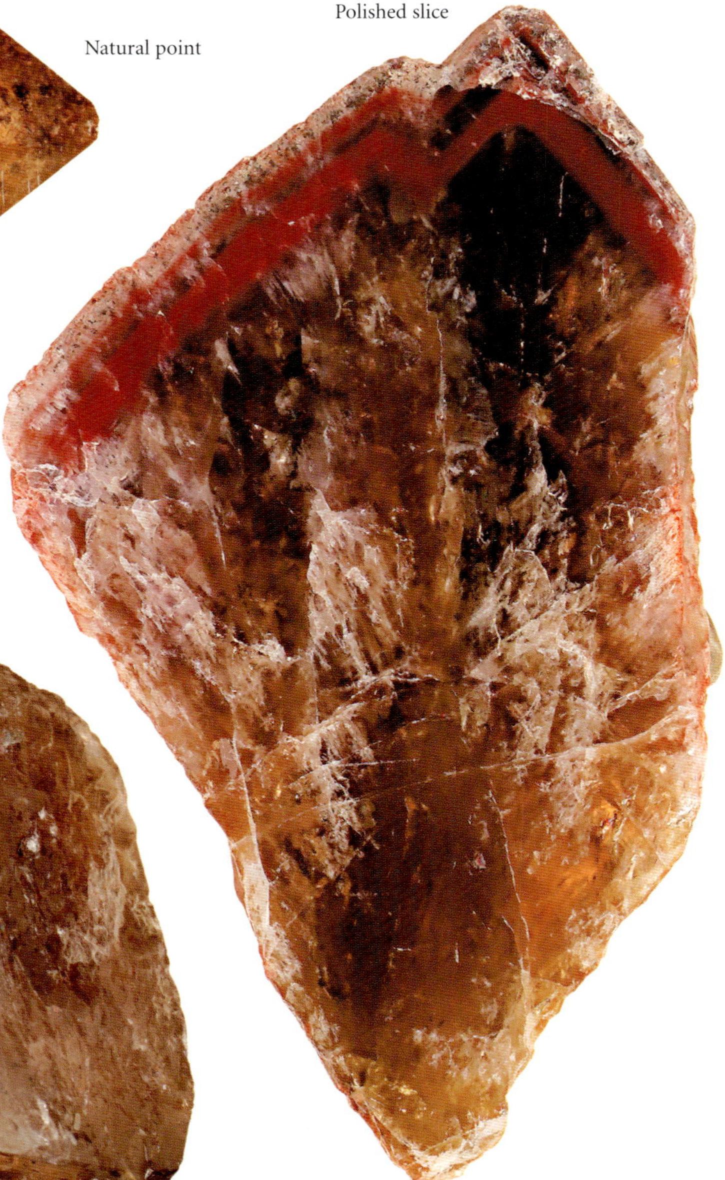

Polished slice

Raw

Glossary

Akashic Record A record that exists beyond time and space containing information on all that has occurred and all that will occur.

Ancestral line The means by which family patterns and beliefs are passed from previous generations.

Angelic realm The energetic level where angels abide.

Ascended Masters Highly evolved spiritual beings who guide the spiritual evolution of the Earth.

Ascension process The means by which people on Earth seek to raise their spiritual and physical vibrations.

Astral travel or journeying The soul is able to leave the physical body behind and travel to distant locations. Also known as out-of-body experience or soul journeying.

Attached entities Spirit forms that become attached to the aura of a living person.

Aura The biomagnetic sheath or etheric body around the physical body, comprising the physical, emotional, mental and spiritual subtle bodies.

Between-lives state The vibratory state in which the soul resides between incarnations.

Cellular memory Cells carry a memory of past-life or ancestral attitudes, trauma and patterns that have become deeply ingrained as on-going negative programmes, such as mortification of the flesh or poverty consciousness, which create dis-ease or are replayed in the present in slightly different forms.

Chakra An energy linkage point between the physical and subtle bodies, seen by a clairvoyant eye as a whirling pool of energy. Malfunction can lead to physical, emotional, mental or spiritual dis-ease or disturbance.

Channelling The process whereby information is passed from a soul not in incarnation to or through an incarnate being on Earth.

Christ consciousness A state in which all life forms of the universe are linked in universal love and awareness, the highest manifestation of divine energy.

Clairaudience Hearing with the psychic ear rather than the physical one, hearing what is inaudible to physical hearing.

Clairvoyance The ability to discern and communicate with spirits.

Cosmic consciousness A very high state of awareness in which the subject is part of universal energy.

Devas Nature spirits, traditionally believed to rule over trees, rivers and mountains.

Dis-ease The state that results from physical imbalances, blocked feelings, suppressed emotions and negative thinking which, if not reversed, will lead to illness.

Earth healing Rectifying the distortion of the Earth's energy field caused by pollution and the destruction of its resources.

Electromagnetic smog A subtle but detectable electromagnetic field given off by power lines and electrical equipment, which can have an adverse effect on sensitive people on the Earth.

Emotional blueprint A subtle energy field carrying the imprint of past- and present-life emotional experiences and attitudes, which influences the present life and may cause psychosomatic dis-ease.

Energy implant Thoughts or negative emotions implanted in the subtle body by outside sources.

Entity Discarnate spirit who hangs around on a plane close to Earth and may attach to an incarnate being.

Entity removal The process of detaching an entity and dispatching it to the appropriate post-death place.

Etheric blueprint The subtle programme from which a physical body is constructed. It carries imprints of past-life dis-ease or injury from which present life illness or disability can result.

Etheric body The subtle biomagnetic sheath surrounding the physical body.

Geode Cave-like crystal that conserves and harnesses energy.

Geopathic stress Earth stress created by energy disturbance from underground water, power lines and ley lines.

Grids/gridding Placing crystals around a building, person or place for energy enhancement or protection – positioning is best dowsed for.

Grounding Creating a strong connection between one's soul, physical body and the Earth.

House clearing Removing entities and negative energies from a house.

Implants Some believe that implants are energies or devices implanted by alien beings, but implants may also be thoughts, blockages or scars created by an outside source in the present or a previous life.

Indigo children Children who are born with a higher vibration to those already on Earth. These children often have extreme difficulty adjusting to the present Earth vibration.

Inner child The part of the personality that remains childlike (but not childish) and innocent, or that may be the repository of abuse and trauma that requires healing.

Inner levels The levels of being that encompass intuition, psychic awareness, emotions, feelings, the subconscious mind and subtle energies.

Journeying Travelling out of the body through the spiritual or other worlds.

Karma of grace When sufficient has been done, or no more can be done, the karma can be released and no longer operates.

Karmic Experiences or on-going lessons arising from a past or present incarnation. Debts, beliefs and emotions such as guilt can be carried over into the present life and create dis-ease but past-life credits and wisdom are available to heal these.

Kundalini An inner, subtle spiritual and sexual creative energy that resides at the base of the spine but can be stimulated to rise to the crown chakra.

Lemuria A very early civilization believed to predate Atlantis.

Mental influences The effect of other people's thoughts and strong opinions on your mind.

Meridian A subtle energy channel that runs close to the surface of the skin, or the planet, that contains acupuncture points.

Metaphysical abilities Abilities such as clairvoyance, telepathy, healing.

Miasm The subtle imprint of an infectious disease or traumatic event from the past that has been passed down through a family or place.

Mortification practices Many monastic orders or religious people undertook practices such as scourging or wearing a hair shirt that were designed to mortify the flesh, ego or spirit and subdue passions and desires. Such practices can lead to or attract psychological mortification or humiliation by yourself or others in the present life.

Multidimensional healing Healing that occurs at multi levels, including but not limited to the physical, cellular, neurological, psychic, emotional, mental, ancestral, karmic, spiritual and higher spiritual, planetary and stellar, terrestrial and extraterrestrial levels, which can travel along a timeline and works on the etheric blueprint of the body, Earth or universe to create total balance and wholeness.

Negative emotional programming 'Oughts' and 'shoulds' and emotions such as guilt that have been instilled, often in childhood or other lives, that remain in the subconscious mind and influence present behaviour, sabotaging efforts to evolve until released.

NLP (neurolinguistic programming) A system for reprogramming the mind and behaviour based on hypnotherapy techniques.

Occlusion or inclusion A mineral deposit within or upon a crystal.

Planetary grid The subtle and invisible Earth energy lines that cover the planet rather like a spider's web.

Pleochroic A crystal appearing to have two or more colours from different angles or light.

Projection Seeking and disliking in others characteristics we cannot accept are actually part of ourselves.

Psychic attack Malevolent thoughts or feelings toward another person, whether consciously or unconsciously directed, that create dis-ease and disruption in that person's life.

Psychic vampirism A person's ability to draw off or 'feed on' the energy of others.

Psychopomp A Greek word for the conductor of a soul through the process of death and into the other world. A psychopomp may be a living person or a spiritual being.

Qi The life force that energizes the physical and subtle bodies.

Radionic A method of diagnosis and treatment at a distance.

Reframing Seeing a past event in a different, more positive light, so that the situation it is creating can be healed.

Reiki A natural hands-on method of healing.

Scry Discerning images in a crystal relating to past, present or future events.

Self The Self encompasses both the incarnated personal self and the non-incarnated higher self (the highest vibration of the overall Self). The higher self can influence and communicate with the personal self. Self is also part of the soul.

Silver cord The subtle link between the physical and etheric body that goes from the third eye of the physical body to the back of the head of the etheric body.

Soul The vehicle for carrying the eternal spirit. *Soul parts* are part of the soul not presently in incarnation, which can include but are not limited to *soul fragments* that split off (see soul retrieval).

Soul group A cluster of souls who have travelled together throughout time, all or some of whom are in incarnation.

Soul links The connections between members of a soul group.

Soulmate A soulmate appears to be an ideal 'other half', a soul partner with whom there is rapport on all levels. However, many soulmate connections carry karma to be dealt with, or difficult soul lessons. Soulmate relationships may not be intended to last a lifetime, nor are they necessarily between sexual partners.

Soul retrieval Trauma, shock or abuse, and even extreme joy, can cause a part of the soul energy to leave and remain stuck at a certain point in life, or past-life death. A soul retrieval practitioner or shaman retrieves the soul, bringing it back for interrogation in the present-life body.

Spirit guides Discarnate beings who work from the between-lives state to provide assistance to those on the Earth.

Spirit releasement Souls can become trapped close to the Earth, spirit releasement sends them home.

Star children Evolved beings from other planetary systems who have incarnated on the Earth to helps its spiritual evolution.

Subtle bodies The layers of the biomagnetic sheath around the physical body.

Subtle energy fields The invisible but detectable energy field that surrounds all living beings.

Thought forms Forms created by strong positive or negative thoughts that can exist on the etheric or spiritual level and affect a person's mental functioning.

Triple burner meridian One of the meridians concerned with temperature control.

Twinflame A soulmate without karma attached. The person with whom you are meant to be in the present life for unconditional mutual support, evolution and love. Spiritual twinflames have often been together in many previous lives.

Index

Acknowledgements

Author Acknowledgements

I am indebted to the work of Melody and other pioneers in discovering and exploring new stones. It is always a joy when the properties reported accord with my own experience with the crystals.

Many people have offered me pointers and personal experiences and in particular I would like to thank Sue and Simon Lilly for their friendship and support. The staff of Earthworks, Poole (www.earthworksuk.com), who loaned some crystals for photography, Clive at Earth Design in Beaminster and David Spiller of Natural Wonders in Swanage have been extremely helpful in sourcing crystals and in sharing their own knowledge of the stones. Dawn Robbins, Jo Evans and Teresa were immensely helpful and great fun to be with when exploring the new crystals. Tina Biles of www.crystalmaster.co.uk was generous in her introduction to Desirite and its properties and sourcing other stones, and John of www.exquisitecrystals.com brought a new vibration into my life with his gift of Flame Aura Spirit Quartz.

Participants on my workshops have also contributed greatly to my knowledge and I send them love and blessings. Jenni Davis did sterling work on research and editing, offering friendship above and beyond the call of duty. Finally, I could not work with crystals and much else besides without Crystal Clear, the ultimate cleansing tool, for which I thank David Eastoe (estoe@yahoo.com).

Picture Acknowledgements

Special photography: © **Octopus Publishing Group Limited**/Andy Komorowski. Other photography: **Octopus Publishing Group Limited**/Mike Prior 10 bottom, 11, 15 left, 15 right; /Unit Photographic 10 top.

Executive Editor Sandra Rigby
Managing Editor Clare Churly
Executive Art Editor Sally Bond
Designer Simon Wilder
Picture Library Manager Jennifer Veall
Production Controller Simone Nauerth